GOLF
RULES
ILLUSTRATED

COMPILED BY
THE UNITED STATES GOLF ASSOCIATION

RULES INCIDENTS BY
GARY A. GALYEAN

**SEQUOYAH REGIONAL LIBRARY SYSTEM
CANTON, GA**

hamlyn

Foreword

Golf is unique in that regardless of where it is played, by amateur or professional, a common set of Rules governs our actions. Golf is played on sport's largest playing field, and no two are identical. It begins with a target, the fairway, that is yards across, and ends with the hole, just 4" in diameter. The obstacles and events that occur in negotiating a golf course demand that the Rules be written in anticipation of the mundane as well as the unusual.

For more than two centuries rules makers have adapted and administered the Rules with the goal of achieving fairness, consistency, and simplicity. Over so much time and so vast a playing field, keeping the Rules as succinct as they are has not been easy.

Appreciating this intricacy, I am pleased to introduce the new Golf Rules Illustrated. This book contains the Rules of Golf effective January 1, 2004 and will be helpful for golfers of all skill levels and all ranges of Rules awareness. The illustrations will help you understand the application of the Rules. The incidents corresponding to the Rules provide examples of rulings at the highest level of competition. As you study these examples and become familiar with them, the procedures will be easier to understand when you encounter them, which will ultimately enhance your enjoyment of the game.

Paul D. Caruso, Jr.
Chairman, Rules of Golf Committee
United States Golf Association

CONTENTS

SECTION 1
ETIQUETTE; BEHAVIOUR ON THE COURSE

INTRODUCTION

This Section provides guidelines on the manner in which the game of golf should be played. If they are followed, all players will gain maximum enjoyment from the game. The overriding principle is that consideration should be shown to others on the course at all times.

THE SPIRIT OF THE GAME

Unlike many sports, golf is played, for the most part, without the supervision of a referee or umpire. The game relies on the integrity of the individual to show consideration for other players and to abide by the Rules. All players should conduct themselves in a disciplined manner, demonstrating courtesy and sportsmanship at all times, irrespective of how competitive they may be. This is the spirit of the game of golf.

SAFETY

Players should ensure that no one is standing close by or in a position to be hit by the club, the ball or any stones, pebbles, twigs or the like when they make a stroke or practice swing.

Players should not play until the players in front are out of range.

Players should always alert greenstaff nearby or ahead when they are about to make a stroke that might endanger them.

If a player plays a ball in a direction where there is a danger of hitting someone, he should immediately shout a warning. The traditional word of warning in such situations is "fore."

CONSIDERATION FOR OTHER PLAYERS

No Disturbance or Distraction Players should always show consideration for other players on the course and should not disturb their play by moving, talking or making unnecessary noise.

Players should ensure that any electronic device taken onto the course does not distract other players.

On the teeing ground, a player should not tee his ball until it is his turn to play.

Players should not stand close to or directly behind the ball, or directly behind the hole, when a player is about to play.

On the putting green On the putting green, players should not stand on another player's line of putt or, when he is making a stroke, cast a shadow over his line of putt.

Players should remain on or close to the putting green until all other players in the group have holed out.

Scoring In stroke play, a player who is acting as a marker should, if necessary, on the way to the next tee, check the score with the player concerned and record it.

PACE OF PLAY

Play at Good Pace and Keep Up Players should play at a good pace. The Committee may establish pace of play guidelines that all players should follow.

It is a group's responsibility to keep up with the group in front. If it loses a clear hole and it is

When taking a practice swing, a player should always make sure that no one is standing where they might be hit.

If a group is holding up the players behind and has lost more than a hole on the players in front, it should invite them to play through.

delaying the group behind, it should invite the group behind to play through, irrespective of the number of players in that group.

Be Ready to Play Players should be ready to play as soon as it is their turn to play. When playing on or near the putting green, they should leave their bags or carts in such a position as will enable quick movement off the green and towards the next tee. When the play of a hole has been completed, players should immediately leave the putting green.

Lost Ball If a player believes his ball may be lost outside a water hazard or is out of bounds, to save time, he should play a provisional ball.

Players searching for a ball should signal the players in the group behind them to play through as soon as it becomes apparent that the ball will not easily be found. They should not search for five minutes before doing so. Having allowed the group behind to play through, they should not continue play until that group has passed and is out of range.

PRIORITY ON THE COURSE

Unless otherwise determined by the Committee, priority on the course is determined by a group's pace of play. Any group playing a whole round is entitled to pass a group playing a shorter round.

CARE OF THE COURSE

Bunkers Before leaving a bunker, players should carefully fill up and smooth over all holes and foot-prints made by them and any nearby made by others. If a rake is within reasonable proximity of the bunker, the rake should be used for this purpose.

Repair of Divots, Ball-Marks and Damage by Shoes Players should carefully repair any divot holes made by them and any damage to the putting green made by the impact of a ball (whether or not made by the player himself). On completion of the hole by all players in the group, damage to the putting green caused by golf shoes should be repaired.

Preventing Unnecessary Damage Players should avoid causing damage to the course by removing divots when taking practice swings or by hitting the head of a club into the ground, whether in anger or for any other reason.

Players should ensure that no damage is done to the putting green when putting down bags or

Always repair divots (top right), carefully repair ball marks on the putting green (bottom left) and smooth over footprints and other marks when leaving a bunker (bottom center). Do not lean on your putter when removing the ball from the hole (middle right).

the flagstick. In order to avoid damaging the hole, players and caddies should not stand too close to the hole and should take care during the handling of the flagstick and the removal of a ball from the hole. The head of a club should not be used to remove a ball from the hole.

Players should not lean on their clubs when on the putting green, particularly when removing the ball from the hole.

The flagstick should be properly replaced in the hole before the players leave the putting green.

Local notices regulating the movement of golf carts should be strictly observed.

CONCLUSION; PENALTIES FOR BREACH

If players follow the guidelines in this Section, it will make the game more enjoyable for everyone.

If a player consistently disregards these guidelines during a round or over a period of time to the detriment of others, it is recommended that the Committee considers taking appropriate disciplinary action against the offending player. Such action may, for example, include prohibiting play for a limited time on the course or in a certain number of competitions. This is considered to be justifiable in terms of protecting the interest of the majority of golfers who wish to play in accordance with these guidelines.

In the case of a serious breach of Etiquette, the Committee may disqualify a player under Rule 33-7.

SECTION 2
DEFINITIONS

ADDRESSING THE BALL

Except in a hazard, a player has addressed the ball when he has taken his stance and grounded his club.

In a bunker or water hazard a player has addressed the ball when he has taken his stance.

The player has decided not to ground his putter. Therefore, he has not "addressed the ball" and cannot be penalized under Rule 18-2b.

Abnormal Ground Conditions An *"abnormal ground condition"* is any *casual water, ground under repair* or hole, cast or runway on the *course* made by a *burrowing animal*, a reptile or a bird.

Addressing the Ball A player has *"addressed the ball"* when he has taken his *stance* and has also grounded his club, except that in a *hazard* a player has *addressed the ball* when he has taken his *stance*.

Advice *"Advice"* is any counsel or suggestion that could influence a player in determining his play, the choice of a club or the method of making a *stroke*.

Information on the *Rules* or on matters of public information, such as the position of *hazards* or the *flagstick* on the *putting green*, is not *advice*.

Ball Deemed to Move See *"Move or Moved."*

Ball Holed See *"Holed."*

Ball Lost See *"Lost Ball."*

Ball in Play A ball is *"in play"* as soon as the player has made a *stroke* on the *teeing ground*. It remains *in play* until it is *holed*, except when it is *lost, out of bounds* or lifted, or another ball has been *substituted* whether or not the substitution is permitted; a ball so *substituted* becomes the *ball in play*.

If a ball is played from outside the *teeing ground* when the player is starting play of a hole, or when attempting to correct this mistake, the ball is not *in play* and Rule 11-4 or 11-5 applies. Otherwise, *ball in play* includes a ball played from outside the *teeing ground* when the player elects or is required to play his next *stroke* from the *teeing ground*.

Exception in match play: *Ball in play* includes a ball played by the player from outside the *teeing ground* when starting play of a hole if the opponent does not require the *stroke* to be cancelled in accordance with Rule 11-4a.

Best-Ball See *"Matches."*

Bunker A *"bunker"* is a *hazard* consisting of a prepared area of ground, often a hollow, from which turf or soil has been removed and replaced with sand or the like.

Grass-covered ground bordering or within a *bunker* including a stacked turf face (whether grass-covered or earthen), is not part of the *bunker*. A wall or lip of the *bunker* not covered with grass is part of the *bunker*.

The margin of a *bunker* extends vertically downwards, but not upwards. A ball is in a *bunker* when it lies in or any part of it touches the *bunker*.

Burrowing Animal A *"burrowing animal"* is an animal that makes a hole for habitation or shelter, such as a rabbit, mole, groundhog, gopher or salamander.

BUNKER

A bunker face consisting of stacked turf (whether grass covered or earthen) is not part of the bunker.

CADDIE

A caddie will carry a player's clubs and offer advice on club selection, the direction of play and line for putting.

CASUAL WATER

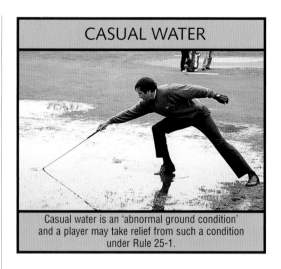

Casual water is an 'abnormal ground condition' and a player may take relief from such a condition under Rule 25-1.

Note: A hole made by a non-burrowing animal, such as a dog, is not an *abnormal ground condition* unless marked or declared as *ground under repair.*

Caddie A "*caddie*" is one who assists the player in accordance with the *Rules*, which may include carrying or handling the player's clubs during play.

When one *caddie* is employed by more than one player, he is always deemed to be the *caddie* of the player whose ball is involved, and *equipment* carried by him is deemed to be that player's *equipment*, except when the *caddie* acts upon specific directions of another player, in which case he is considered to be that other player's *caddie*.

Casual Water "*Casual water*" is any temporary accumulation of water on the *course* that is visible before or after the player takes his *stance* and is not in a *water hazard*. Snow and natural ice, other than frost, are either *casual water* or *loose impediments*, at the option of the player. Manufactured ice is an *obstruction*. Dew and frost are not *casual water*. A ball is in *casual water* when it lies in or any part of it touches the *casual water*.

Committee The "*Committee*" is the committee in charge of the competition or, if the matter does not arise in a competition, the committee in charge of the *course*.

Competitor A "*competitor*" is a player in a stroke play competition. A "*fellow-competitor*" is any person with whom the *competitor* plays. Neither is *partner* of the other.

In stroke play *foursome* and *four-ball* competitions, where the context so admits, the word "*competitor*" or "*fellow-competitor*" includes his *partner*.

EQUIPMENT

Equipment includes a golf cart. As it is not being moved by one of the players, the cart and everything in it are deemed to be the equipment of the player whose ball is involved.

GROUND UNDER REPAIR

Course The "*course*" is the whole area within any boundaries established by the *Committee* (see Rule 33-2).

Equipment "*Equipment*" is anything used, worn or carried by or for the player except any ball he has played at the hole being played and any small object, such as a coin or a *tee*, when used to mark the position of a ball or the extent of an area in which a ball is to be dropped. *Equipment* includes a golf cart, whether or not motorized. If such a cart is shared by two or more players, the cart and everything in it are deemed to be the *equipment* of the player whose ball is involved except that, when the cart is being moved by one of the players sharing it, the cart and everything in it are deemed to be that player's *equipment*.

Note: A ball played at the hole being played is *equipment* when it has been lifted and not put back *into play*.

Fellow-Competitor See "*Competitor*."

Flagstick The "*flagstick*" is a movable straight indicator, with or without bunting or other material attached, centered in the *hole* to show its position. It must be circular in cross-section. Padding or shock absorbent material that might unduly influence the movement of the ball is prohibited.

Forecaddie A "*forecaddie*" is one who is employed by the *Committee* to indicate to players the position of balls during play. He is an *outside agency*.

Four-Ball See "*Matches.*"

Foursome See "*Matches.*"

Ground Under Repair "*Ground under repair*" is any part of the course so marked by order of the *Committee* or so declared by its authorized representative. It includes material piled for removal and a hole made by a greenkeeper, even if not so marked.

All ground and any grass, bush, tree or other

growing thing within the *ground under repair* is part of the *ground under repair*. The margin of *ground under repair* extends vertically downwards, but not upwards. Stakes and lines defining *ground under repair* are in such ground. Such stakes are *obstructions*. A ball is in *ground under repair* when it lies in or any part of it touches the *ground under repair*.

Note 1: Grass cuttings and other material left on the *course* that have been abandoned and are not intended to be removed are not *ground under repair* unless so marked.

Note 2: The *Committee* may make a Local Rule prohibiting play from *ground under repair* or an environmentally-sensitive area defined as *ground under repair*.

Hazards   A "*hazard*" is any *bunker* or *water hazard*.

Hole   The "*hole*" must be 4¼ inches (108 mm) in diameter and at least 4 inches (101.6 mm)

deep. If a lining is used, it must be sunk at least 1 inch (25.4 mm) below the *putting green* surface unless the nature of the soil makes it impracticable to do so; its outer diameter must not exceed 4¼ inches (108 mm).

Holed   A ball is "*holed*" when it is at rest within the circumference of the *hole* and all of it is below the level of the lip of the *hole*.

Honor   The player who is to play first from the *teeing ground* is said to have the "*honor*".

Lateral Water Hazard   A "*lateral water hazard*" is a *water hazard* or that part of a *water hazard* so situated that it is not possible or is deemed by the *Committee* to be impracticable to drop a ball behind the *water hazard* in accordance with Rule 26-1b.

That part of a *water hazard* to be played as a *lateral water hazard* should be distinctively marked. A ball is in a *lateral water hazard* when

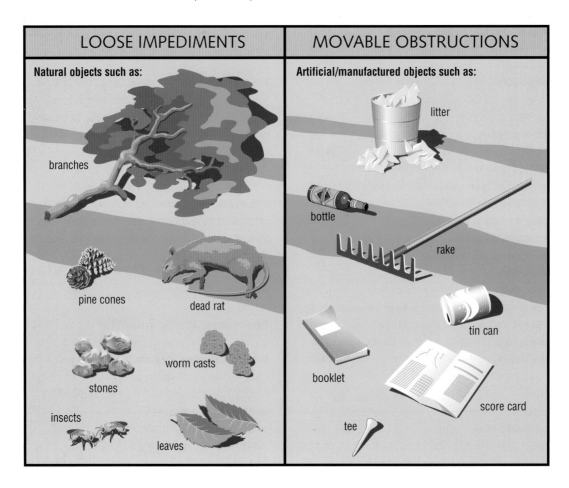

LOOSE IMPEDIMENTS

Natural objects such as:

branches

pine cones

dead rat

stones

worm casts

insects

leaves

MOVABLE OBSTRUCTIONS

Artificial/manufactured objects such as:

litter

bottle

rake

tin can

booklet

score card

tee

it lies in or any part of it touches the *lateral water hazard*.

Note 1: Stakes or lines used to define a *lateral water hazard* must be red. When both stakes and lines are used to define *lateral water hazards*, the stakes identify the *hazard* and the lines define the *hazard* margin.

Note 2: The *Committee* may make a Local Rule prohibiting play from an environmentally-sensitive area defined as a *lateral water hazard*.

Note 3: The *Committee* may define a *lateral water hazard* as a *water hazard*.

Line of Play The "*line of play*" is the direction that the player wishes his ball to take after a *stroke*, plus a reasonable distance on either side of the intended direction. The *line of play* extends vertically upward from the ground, but does not extend beyond the *hole*.

Line of Putt The "*line of putt*" is the line that the player wishes his ball to take after a *stroke* on the *putting green*. Except with respect to Rule 16-1e, the *line of putt* includes a reasonable distance on either side of the intended line. The *line of putt* does not extend beyond the *hole*.

Loose Impediments "*Loose impediments*" are natural objects, including:
- stones, leaves, twigs, branches and the like,
- dung, and
- worms and insects and the casts and heaps made by them,

provided they are not:
- fixed or growing,
- solidly embedded, or
- adhering to the ball

Sand and loose soil are *loose impediments* on the *putting green*, but not elsewhere.

Snow and natural ice, other than frost, are either *casual water* or *loose impediments* at the option of the player.

Dew and frost are not *loose impediments*.

Lost Ball A ball is deemed "*lost*" if:
a. It is not found or identified as his by the player within five minutes after the player's *side* or his or their *caddies* have begun to search for it; or

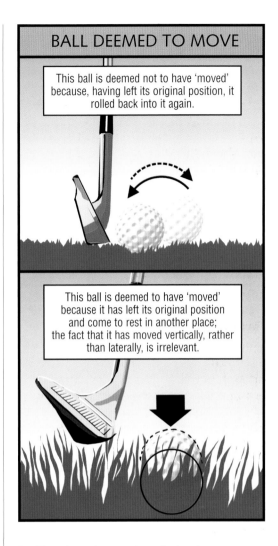

BALL DEEMED TO MOVE

This ball is deemed not to have 'moved' because, having left its original position, it rolled back into it again.

This ball is deemed to have 'moved' because it has left its original position and come to rest in another place; the fact that it has moved vertically, rather than laterally, is irrelevant.

b. The player has made a *stroke* at a *substituted ball*; or

c. The player has made a *stroke* at a *provisional ball* from the place where the original ball is likely to be or from a point nearer the *hole* than that place.

Time spent in playing a *wrong ball* is not counted in the five-minute period allowed for search.

Marker A "*marker*" is one who is appointed by the *Committee* to record a *competitor's* score in stroke play. He may be a *fellow-competitor*. He is not a *referee*.

Matches
Single: A match in which one plays against another.
Threesome: A match in which one plays against

11

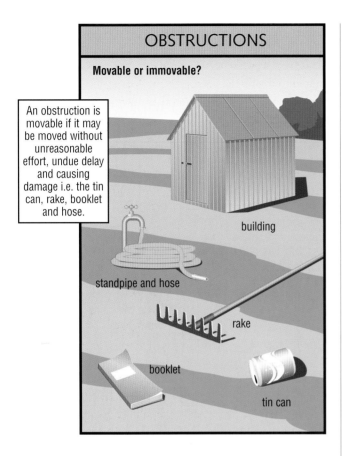

OBSTRUCTIONS

Movable or immovable?

An obstruction is movable if it may be moved without unreasonable effort, undue delay and causing damage i.e. the tin can, rake, booklet and hose.

standpipe and hose

rake

booklet

building

tin can

two, and each *side* plays one ball.

Foursome: A match in which two play against two, and each *side* plays one ball.

Three-Ball: A match play competition in which three play against one another, each playing his own ball. Each player is playing two distinct *matches*.

Best-Ball: A match in which one plays against the better ball of two or the best ball of three players.

Four-Ball: A match in which two play their better ball against the better ball of two other players.

Move or Moved A ball is deemed to have "*moved*" if it leaves its position and comes to rest in any other place.

Nearest Point of Relief The "*nearest point of relief*" is the reference point for taking relief without penalty from interference by an immovable *obstruction* (Rule 24-2), an *abnormal ground condition* (Rule 25-1) or a *wrong putting green* (Rule 25-3).

It is the point on the *course* nearest to where the ball lies:

(i) that is not nearer the *hole*, and

(ii) where, if the ball were so positioned, no interference by the condition from which relief is sought would exist for the *stroke* the player would have made from the original position if the condition were not there.

Note: In order to determine the *nearest point of relief* accurately, the player should use the club with which he would have made his next *stroke* if the condition were not there to simulate the *address* position, direction of play and swing for such a *stroke*.

Observer An "*observer*" is one who is appointed by the *Committee* to assist a *referee* to decide questions of fact and to report to him any breach of a *Rule*. An *observer* should not attend the *flagstick*, stand at or mark the position of the *hole*, or lift the ball or mark its position.

Obstructions An "*obstruction*" is anything artificial, including the artificial surfaces and sides of roads and paths and manufactured ice, except:

a. Objects defining *out of bounds*, such as walls, fences, stakes and railings;

b. Any part of an immovable artificial object that is *out of bounds*; and

c. Any construction declared by the *Committee* to be an integral part of the *course*.

An *obstruction* is a movable *obstruction* if it may be moved without unreasonable effort, without unduly delaying play and without causing damage. Otherwise it is an immovable *obstruction*.

Note: The *Committee* may make a Local Rule declaring a movable *obstruction* to be an immovable *obstruction*.

Out of Bounds "*Out of bounds*" is beyond the boundaries of the *course* or any part of the *course* so marked by the *Committee*.

When *out of bounds* is defined by reference to stakes or a fence or as being beyond stakes or a fence, the *out of bounds* line is determined by the nearest inside points of the stakes or fence posts at ground level excluding angled supports.

PARTNER

A partner is a player associated with another player on the same side.

Objects defining *out of bounds* such as walls, fences, stakes and railings, are not *obstructions* and are deemed to be fixed.

When *out of bounds* is defined by a line on the ground, the line itself is *out of bounds*.

The *out of bounds* line extends vertically upwards and downwards.

A ball is *out of bounds* when all of it lies *out of bounds*.

A player may stand *out of bounds* to play a ball lying within bounds.

Outside Agency An *"outside agency"* is any agency not part of the match or, in stroke play, not part of the *competitor's side*, and includes a *referee*, a *marker*, an *observer* and a *forecaddie*. Neither wind nor water is an *outside agency*.

Partner A *"partner"* is a player associated with another player on the same *side*.

In a *threesome*, *foursome*, *best-ball* or *four-ball* match, where the context so admits, the word *"player"* includes his *partner* or *partners*.

Penalty Stroke A *"penalty stroke"* is one added to the score of a player or *side* under certain *Rules*. In a *threesome* or *foursome*, *penalty strokes* do not affect the order of play.

Provisional Ball A *"provisional ball"* is a ball played under Rule 27-2 for a ball that may be *lost* outside a *water hazard* or may be *out of bounds*.

Putting Green The *"putting green"* is all ground of the hole being played that is specially prepared for putting or otherwise defined as such by the *Committee*. A ball is on the *putting green* when any part of it touches the *putting green*.

Referee A *"referee"* is one who is appointed by the *Committee* to accompany players to decide questions of fact and apply the *Rules*. He must act on any breach of a *Rule* that he observes or is reported to him.

A *referee* should not attend the *flagstick*, stand at or mark the position of the *hole*, or lift the ball or mark its position.

Rub of the Green A *"rub of the green"* occurs when a ball in motion is accidentally deflected or stopped by any *outside agency* (see Rule 19-1).

Rule or Rules The term *"Rule"* includes:
a. The Rules of Golf and their interpretations as contained in "Decisions on the Rules of Golf";
b. Any Conditions of Competition established by the *Committee* under Rule 33-1 and Appendix I;
c. Any Local Rules established by the *Committee* under Rule 33-8a and Appendix I; and
d. The specifications on clubs and the ball in Appendices II and III.

Side
A *"side"* is a player, or two or more players who are *partners*.

Single See "*Matches.*"

Stance Taking the "*stance*" consists in a player placing his feet in position for and preparatory to making a *stroke*.

Stipulated Round The "*stipulated round*" consists of playing the holes of the *course* in their correct sequence unless otherwise authorized by the *Committee*.

The number of holes in a *stipulated round* is 18 unless a smaller number is authorized by the *Committee*. As to extension of *stipulated round* in match play, see Rule 2-3.

Stroke A "*stroke*" is the forward movement of the club made with the intention of striking at and moving the ball, but if a player checks his downswing voluntarily before the clubhead reaches the ball he has not made a *stroke*.

Substituted Ball A "*substituted ball*" is a ball put into play for the original ball that was either *in play, lost, out of bounds* or lifted.

Tee A "*tee*" is a device designed to raise the ball off the ground. It must not be longer than 4 inches (101.6 mm) and it must not be designed or manufactured in such a way that it could indicate the *line of play* or influence the movement of the ball.

Teeing Ground The "*teeing ground*" is the starting place for the hole to be played. It is a rectangular area two club-lengths in depth, the front and the sides of which are defined by the outside limits of two tee-markers. A ball is outside the *teeing ground* when all of it lies outside the *teeing ground*.

Three-Ball See "*Matches.*"

Threesomes See "*Matches.*"

Through the Green "*Through the green*" is the whole area of the *course* except:

a. The *teeing ground* and *putting green* of the hole being played; and

b. All *hazards* on the *course*.

Water Hazard A "*water hazard*" is any sea, lake, pond, river, ditch, surface drainage ditch or other open water course (whether or not containing water) and anything of a similar nature on the *course*.

All ground or water within the margin of a *water hazard* is part of the *water hazard*. The margin of a *water hazard* extends vertically upwards and downwards. Stakes and lines defining the margins of *water hazards* are in the *hazards*. Such stakes are *obstructions*. A ball is in a *water hazard* when it lies in or any part of it touches the *water hazard*.

Note 1: Stakes or lines used to define a *water hazard* must be yellow. When both stakes and lines are used to define *water hazards*, the stakes identify the *hazard* and the lines define the *hazard* margin.

Note 2: The *Committee* may make a Local Rule prohibiting play from an environmentally-sensitive area defined as a *water hazard*.

Wrong Ball A "*wrong ball*" is any ball other than the player's:

- *ball in play*;
- *provisional ball*; or
- second ball played under Rule 3-3 or Rule 20-7c in stroke play; and includes
- another player's ball;
- an abandoned ball; and
- the player's original ball when it is no longer *in play*

Note: *Ball in play* includes a ball *substituted* for the *ball in play*, whether or not the substitution is permitted.

Wrong Putting Green A "*wrong putting green*" is any *putting green* other than that of the hole being played. Unless otherwise prescribed by the *Committee*, this term includes a practice *putting green* or pitching green on the *course*.

DEFINITION OF A STROKE

At this point, as the player has not started his downswing, he has not begun his stroke. Once the player begins his downswing he is considered to have made a stroke, unless he checks his downswing voluntarily.

TEEING GROUND

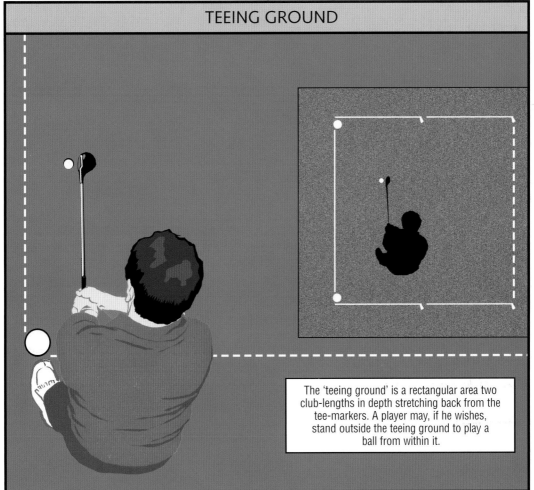

The 'teeing ground' is a rectangular area two club-lengths in depth stretching back from the tee-markers. A player may, if he wishes, stand outside the teeing ground to play a ball from within it.

15

SECTION 3
THE RULES OF PLAY

RULE **1** | **THE GAME**

DEFINITIONS

All defined terms are in *italics* and are listed alphabetically in the Definitions section – see pages 6–15.

1-1. GENERAL
The Game of Golf consists of playing a ball with a club from the *teeing ground* into the *hole* by a *stroke* or successive *strokes* in accordance with the *Rules*.

1-2. EXERTING INFLUENCE ON BALL
A player or *caddie* must not take any action to influence the position or the movement of a ball except in accordance with the *Rules*.
(Removal of movable *obstruction* – see Rule 24-1)

PENALTY FOR BREACH OF RULE 1-2:
Match play – Loss of hole; Stroke play – Two strokes.
Note: In the case of a serious breach of Rule 1-2, the *Committee* may impose a penalty of disqualification.

MATCH PLAY: AGREEMENT TO CONSIDER HOLE HALVED

How about a half?

Good idea, let's move on to the next hole.

An agreement to halve a hole being played is not an agreement to waive the Rules.

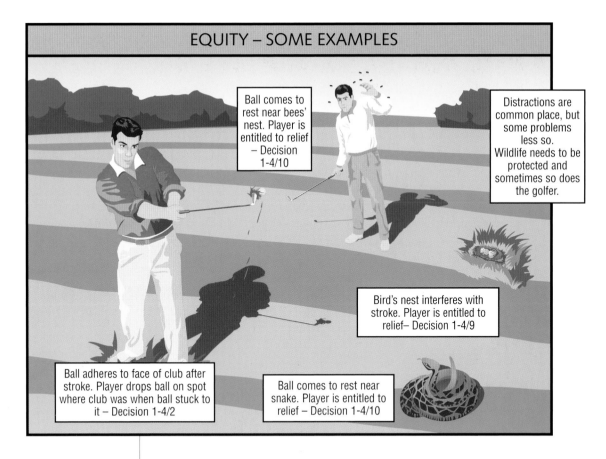

EQUITY – SOME EXAMPLES

Ball comes to rest near bees' nest. Player is entitled to relief – Decision 1-4/10

Distractions are common place, but some problems less so. Wildlife needs to be protected and sometimes so does the golfer.

Bird's nest interferes with stroke. Player is entitled to relief– Decision 1-4/9

Ball adheres to face of club after stroke. Player drops ball on spot where club was when ball stuck to it – Decision 1-4/2

Ball comes to rest near snake. Player is entitled to relief – Decision 1-4/10

1-3. AGREEMENT TO WAIVE RULES

Players must not agree to exclude the operation of any *Rule* or to waive any penalty incurred.

PENALTY FOR BREACH OF RULE 1-3:

Match play – Disqualification of both sides;

Stroke play – Disqualification of competitors concerned.

(Agreeing to play out of turn in stroke play – see Rule 10-2c)

1-4. POINTS NOT COVERED BY RULES

See **incident** involving Rule 1-4 below

If any point in dispute is not covered by the *Rules*, the decision should be made in accordance with equity.

RULE 1 INCIDENT

No good deed goes unpunished, or so it might have seemed to Brett Quigley and Dan Forsman when they were disqualified following the third round of the 2002 Bay Hill Invitational.

At the 18th hole, Quigley's ball was embedded in the rough and he was entitled to relief as provided under the Local Rule adopted by the PGA Tour. After his first drop, the ball came to rest in a bunker requiring him to re-drop. [Rule 20-2c(i).]

After the second drop, the ball again rolled toward the bunker. This time, however, in an attempt to be helpful, Forsman's caddie – an outside agency by definition – stopped the ball before it came to rest. Realizing that something was amiss, Quigley erroneously thought Forsman's caddie's action had invalidated his second drop and that he should drop again, which he did.

In fact, Quigley should have placed the ball where it was stopped by the outside agency. [Rule 19-1.]

Although unrealized by Quigley, playing from the spot of his redrop resulted in a two-stroke penalty for playing a stroke from a wrong place [Rule 20-7b.] Unrealized by Forsman, was a two-stroke penalty for his caddie's intentional effort to exert influence on Quigley's ball [Rule 1-2, 6-4, Note under 19-1.]

Unfortunately, both players assumed the situation had been rectified when Quigley re-dropped for the third time. Never intending to evade the Rules, neither were they aware that they both had incurred a violation. Their scorecards were submitted without the required penalty strokes. Their mistakes were discovered later, and they were both disqualified for returning a scorecard with a score lower than they had actually taken. [Rule 6-6d.]

RULE **MATCH PLAY**

DEFINITIONS | All defined terms are in *italics* and are listed alphabetically in the Definitions section – see pages 6–15.

2-1. GENERAL

A match consists of one *side* playing against another over a *stipulated round* unless otherwise decreed by the *Committee*.

In match play the game is played by holes.

Except as otherwise provided in the *Rules*, a hole is won by the *side* that *holes* its ball in the fewer *strokes*. In a handicap match the lower net score wins the hole.

The state of the match is expressed by the terms: so many "holes up" or "all square" and so many "to play."

A *side* is "dormie" when it is as many holes up as there are holes remaining to be played.

2-2. HALVED HOLE

A hole is halved if each *side holes* out in the same number of *strokes*. When a player has *holed* out and his opponent has been left with a *stroke* for the half, if the player subsequently incurs a penalty, the hole is halved.

2-3. WINNER OF MATCH

A match is won when one *side* leads by a number of holes greater than the number remaining to be played.

If there is a tie, the *Committee* may extend the *stipulated round* by as many holes as are required for a match to be won.

WINNER OF MATCH: HOLE-BY-HOLE PLAY-OFF

Good putt. That squares the match. We'll have to go back to the 1st for a sudden death play-off.

No. We started this match at the 10th hole, so that is our first extra hole. As before you'll get your handicap stroke.

See **incident** involving Rule 2-4 on page 20–21

2-4. CONCESSION OF NEXT STROKE, HOLE OR MATCH

A player may concede his opponent's next *stroke* at any time provided the opponent's ball is at rest. The opponent is considered to have *holed* out with his next *stroke* and the ball may be removed by either *side*.

A player may concede a hole at any time prior to the start or conclusion of that hole.

A player may concede a match at any time prior to the start or conclusion of that match.

A concession may not be declined or withdrawn.

(Ball overhanging *hole* – see Rule 16-2)

2-5. DOUBT AS TO PROCEDURE; DISPUTES AND CLAIMS

In match play, if a doubt or dispute arises between the players, a player may make a claim. If no duly authorized representative of the *Committee* is available within a reasonable time, the players must continue the match without delay. The *Committee* may consider a claim only if the player making the claim notifies his opponent (i) that he is making a claim, (ii) of the

19

facts of the situation and (iii) that he wants a ruling. The claim must be made before any player in the match plays from the next *teeing ground* or, in the case of the last hole of the match, before all players in the match leave the *putting green*.

A later claim may not be considered by the *Committee* unless it is based on facts previously unknown to the player making the claim and he had been given wrong information (Rules 6-2a and 9) by an opponent.

Once the result of the match has been officially announced, a later claim may not be considered by the *Committee* unless it is satisfied that the opponent knew he was giving wrong information.

2-6. GENERAL PENALTY

The penalty for a breach of a *Rule* in match play is loss of hole except when otherwise provided.

RULE 2 INCIDENTS

Jack Nicklaus' concession of Tony Jacklin's putt on the final hole during the final match of the 1969 Ryder Cup resulted in this match play event's first tie, and is hailed as one of golf's finest acts of sportsmanship. Pierre Fulke's offer of a half to Davis Love on the final hole of the 2002 Ryder Cup was equally magnanimous.

In 1969, going into the final day's competition at the Royal Birkdale Golf Club in Southport, England, the United States and Great Britain were tied at eight points apiece. That morning's singles matches resulted in a two-point lead by the British, which was reciprocated by the U.S. in the afternoon. This left the matches tied at 15 ½ with only the final match of Nicklaus and Jacklin still on the course. Eighteen of the 32 Ryder Cup matches went to the final hole that year, and it was there that the three-day competition would be ultimately decided.

Nicklaus had the upper hand, as Jacklin had fallen behind on the back nine. As the reigning British Open Champion, Jacklin would not relent. Indeed, he eagled the 17th to go all square with Nicklaus.

As the defending champions after their victory in 1967 at Champions Golf Club in Houston, the U.S. team needed only a tie at the last hole to tie the overall competition, which would ensure that the cup remained with the U.S. team.

At the par-5 18th, Jacklin missed his putt for birdie. Nicklaus holed his four-footer for par. Jacklin was left with a short putt to tie. If he holed the putt, it would be the first time the Ryder Cup had ended in a tie. A miss by Jacklin would result in an outright win by the Americans.

Before Jacklin could putt, Nicklaus picked up Jacklin's marker, conceding the Englishman's putt and ensuring the tie. "I don't think you would have missed that Tony," Nicklaus reportedly said, "but under these circumstances I'd never give you the opportunity."

"The length of the putt has varied after 30 years," Jacklin has said. "It's been as long as four feet. But my recollection is 20 inches. Of course, I could have missed it; there are no guarantees in golf, especially in the crucible of the Ryder Cup, but I believe I would have made it. But Jack saw the big picture. Two months before I had become the first British player in 18 years to win the British Open, so there was very much a pro-British fervor at the Ryder Cup in England that year. Jack saw that the putt on the last hole in 1969 meant a heck of a lot more to the Ryder Cup than who won or lost that particular match. It was a great moment."

Thirty-three years later, the larger picture that Jacklin alluded to in 1969 had come to pass. The 2002 Ryder Cup was decided in favor of the European team when Paul McGinley holed a six-foot putt on The Belfry's 18th hole to halve his match with Jim Furyk. The tie's half point split to each team gave Europe 14 ½ points and a winning margin.

The European team ran to embrace McGinley and the 35,000 spectators began the celebration with three matches still on the course.

All square in the 18th fairway, Davis Love III and Pierre Fulke watched the mayhem on the green. Sergio Garcia ran across the green and then down the 18th fairway. Contemplating the scene before him and sensing Love's distraction with Garcia's actions, Fulke offered Love a half at the 18th without completing the hole.

"I asked our match referee, Andy McFee, if it was okay if we just halved it there and then," Love said. "He said, 'Well, okay, but it's not good form. You can do whatever you want though.'"

"We didn't need to play with people on the fairway," Love said later. "…Pierre Fulke is one of the classiest players I've ever been around for 18 holes. He offered me a half point, and I took him up on the offer, and that's the way the match is."

RULE **STROKE PLAY**

DEFINITIONS

All defined terms are in *italics* and are listed alphabetically in the Definitions section – see pages 6–15.

3-1. WINNER

The *competitor* who plays the *stipulated round* or rounds in the fewest *strokes* is the winner.

In a handicap competition, the *competitor* with the lowest net score for the *stipulated round* or rounds is the winner.

3-2. FAILURE TO HOLE OUT

If a *competitor* fails to hole out at any hole and does not correct his mistake before he makes a *stroke* on the next *teeing ground* or, in the case of the last hole of the round, before he leaves the *putting green*, **he is disqualified**.

3-3. DOUBT AS TO PROCEDURE
a. Procedure

In stroke play, if a *competitor* is doubtful of his rights or the correct procedure during play of a hole he may, without penalty, complete the hole with two balls.

After the doubtful situation has arisen and before taking further action, the *competitor* must announce to his *marker* or a *fellow-competitor* that he

DOUBT AS TO PROCEDURE IN STROKE PLAY

intends to play two balls and which ball he wishes to count if the *Rules* permit. If he fails to do so, the provisions of Rule 3-3b(ii) apply.

The *competitor* must report the facts of the situation to the *Committee* before returning his score card. If he fails to do so, **he is disqualified**.

b. Determination of Score for Hole

(i)   If the ball that the *competitor* selected in advance to count has been played in accordance with the *Rules*, the score with that ball is the *competitor's* score for the hole. Otherwise, the score with the other ball counts if the *Rules* allow the procedure adopted for that ball.

(ii) If the *competitor* fails to announce in advance his decision to complete the hole with two balls, or which ball he wishes to count, the score with the original ball counts, provided it has been played in accordance with the *Rules*. If the original ball is not one of the ball being played, the first ball put into play counts, provided it has been played in accordance with the *Rules*. Otherwise, the score with the other ball counts if the *Rules* allow the procedure adopted for that ball.

Note 1: If a *competitor* plays a second ball under Rule 3-3, the *strokes* made after this Rule has been invoked with the ball ruled not to count and *penalty strokes* incurred solely by playing that ball are disregarded.

Note 2: A second ball played under Rule 3-3 is not a *provisional ball* under Rule 27-2.

3-4. REFUSAL TO COMPLY WITH A RULE

If a *competitor* refuses to comply with a *Rule* affecting the rights of another *competitor*, **he is disqualified**.

3-5. GENERAL PENALTY

The penalty for a breach of a *Rule* in stroke play is two strokes except when otherwise provided.

RULE 3 BACKGROUND

Match play came first to golf. One played against another, one hole and one match at a time. Then, sometimes, two might play against two, or maybe two played against one. Whatever the configuration, the match being played was that match's total universe until it was decided. Putts, holes and matches could be conceded. If you lay 2 beside the hole and your opponent lay 9, he could give you the hole and you walked to the next tee. If your opponents were too ill to play, they could give you the match.

By the mid-18th century, when golf clubs were being formed in Scotland, their members desired a different form of competition in which the total number of strokes taken to play a course would be counted. On May 9, 1759 the Society of St. Andrews Golfers resolved "… whoever puts in the Ball at the fewest Strokes Over the Field, being 22 Holes, Shall be Declared and Sustain Victor." The victor was often awarded a medal from which the term "medal play" finds its origin.

During stroke play a few things, which had been decided by loss of hole in match play, needed more precise direction. These Rules remain today. For instance, all balls must be holed out in stroke play. Without such a stipulation, a player's round is incomplete and the score incomparable to those who have holed out. The player now, as then, is disqualified if he does not hole out, because he has not completed the course.

To ensure that everyone plays the same course, tee-markers take on added importance in stroke play. Beginning a hole from outside the markers results in a two-stroke penalty and a ball must be played from within their boundaries. Just as all players must end in the same place, they must also begin in the same place. Failure to correct an error of this type also results in disqualification.

Another important distinction is the method used when doubt arises about how to proceed. Rule 3-3 allows those competing in stroke play to play a second ball. The player must announce ahead of time his intent to play a second ball and which ball he wishes to use should the Rules allow it. In match play, playing a second ball is not permitted. Rather, the player must make a specific claim if he objects to an action taken by his opponent before anyone plays from the next teeing ground.

Because the total number of strokes determines the winner in stroke play, the score card becomes each player's testament to what he has accomplished on the course, and a marker must attest it. Errors in scorekeeping cannot be tolerated when the best score is what determines the winner. Thus, a score for a hole that is recorded higher than actually taken can be included because it would not create an advantage, but a lower score must result in disqualification because it would create one.

The responsibility for violations in both forms of play rests with the players themselves. However, a loss of hole penalty in match play can be assessed and the match continued. While there are 15 one-stroke penalties that apply to both forms of play, the general penalty in stroke play is two strokes and play continues. However, a stroke play violation that results in a serious inequity between a player's procedure and that of the entire field must logically result in disqualification.

RULE CLUBS

CLUBS AND THE BALL

The United States Golf Association (USGA) reserves the right, at any time, to change the Rules and make or change the interpretations relating to clubs and balls (see Appendices II and III).

A player in doubt as to the conformity of a club should consult the USGA. A manufacturer should submit to the USGA a sample of a club to be manufactured for a ruling as to whether the club conforms with the *Rules*. If a manufacturer fails to submit a sample or to await a ruling before manufacturing and/or marketing the club, the manufacturer assumes the risk of a ruling that the club does not conform with the *Rules*. Any sample submitted to the USGA will become its property for reference purposes.

DEFINITIONS All defined terms are in *italics* and are listed alphabetically in the Definitions section – see pages 6–15.

4-1. FORM AND MAKE OF CLUBS
a. General
The player's clubs must conform with this Rule and the provisions, specifications and interpretations set forth in Appendix II.

b. Wear and Alteration
A club that conforms with the *Rules* when new is deemed to conform after wear through normal use. Any part of a club that has been purposely altered is regarded as new and must, in its altered state, conform with the *Rules*.

4-2. PLAYING CHARACTERISTICS CHANGED AND FOREIGN MATERIAL
a. Playing Characteristics Changed
During a *stipulated round*, the playing characteristics of a club must not be purposely changed by adjustment or by any other means.

b. Foreign Material
Foreign material must not be applied to the club face for the purpose of influencing the movement of the ball.

PENALTY FOR BREACH OF RULE 4-1 OR 4-2:
Disqualification.

4-3. DAMAGED CLUBS: REPAIR AND REPLACEMENT
a. Damage in Normal Course of Play
If, during a *stipulated round*, a player's club is damaged in the normal course of play, he may:

CLUB UNFIT FOR PLAY

If a player's club is damaged in the normal course of play (e.g. in playing a stroke or in taking a practice swing) rendering it unfit for play, the player may, without unduly delaying play, repair it or have it repaired or replace the damaged club with any club. However, he may not borrow a club being used by anyone playing on the course.

When a club is damaged other than in the normal course of play it may not be used during the remainder of the round. Ben Crenshaw became more familiar with the provisions of Rule 4-3b at the 1987 Ryder Cup match. See the story on page 28.

(i) use the club in its damaged state for the remainder of the *stipulated round*; or

(ii) without unduly delaying play, repair it or have it repaired; or

(iii) as an additional option available only if the club is unfit for play, replace the damaged club with any club. The replacement of a club must not unduly delay play and must not be made by borrowing any club selected for play by any other person playing on the *course*.

PENALTY FOR BREACH OF RULE 4-3a:
See Penalty Statement for Rule 4-4a, b, and c.

Note: A club is unfit for play if it is substantially damaged, e.g., the shaft is dented, significantly bent or breaks into pieces; the clubhead becomes loose, detached or significantly deformed; or the grip becomes loose. A club is not unfit for play solely because the club's lie or loft has been altered, or the clubhead is scratched.

b. Damage Other Than in Normal Course of Play

See **incident** involving Rule 4-3b on page 28

If, during a *stipulated round*, a player's club is damaged other than in the normal course of play rendering it non-conforming or changing its playing characteristics, the club must not subsequently be used or replaced during the round.

c. Damage Prior to Round

A player may use a club damaged prior to a round provided the club, in its damaged state, conforms with the *Rules*.

Damage to a club that occurred prior to a round may be repaired during the round, provided the playing characteristics are not changed and play is not unduly delayed.

PENALTY FOR BREACH OF RULE 4-3b or c:
Disqualification.

(Undue delay – see Rule 6-7)

4-4. MAXIMUM OF FOURTEEN CLUBS
a. Selection and Addition of Clubs

See **incident** involving Rule 4-4a below

The player must not start a *stipulated round* with more than fourteen clubs. He is limited to the clubs thus selected for that round except that, if he started with fewer than fourteen clubs, he may add any number provided his total number does not exceed fourteen.

The addition of a club or clubs must not unduly delay play (Rule 6-7) and the player must not add or borrow any club selected for play by any other person playing on the *course*.

b. Partners May Share Clubs
Partners may share clubs, provided that the total number of clubs carried by the *partners* so sharing does not exceed fourteen.

PENALTY FOR BREACH OF RULE 4-4a or b,
REGARDLESS OF NUMBER OF EXCESS CLUBS CARRIED:
Match play – At the conclusion of the hole at which the breach is discovered, the state of the match is adjusted by deducting one hole for each hole at which a breach occurred. Maximum deduction per round: Two holes. Stroke play – Two strokes for each hole at which any breach occurred; maximum penalty per round: Four strokes. Bogey and par competitions – Penalties as in match play. Stableford competitions – see Note 1 to Rule 32-1b.

c. Excess Club Declared Out of Play
Any club or clubs carried or used in breach of Rule 4-3a(iii) or Rule 4-4 must be declared out of play by the player to his opponent in match play or his *marker* or a *fellow-competitor* in stroke play immediately upon discovery that a breach has occurred. The player must not use the club or clubs for the remainder of the *stipulated round*.

PENALTY FOR BREACH OF RULE 4-4c:
Disqualification.

RULE 4 INCIDENT

It is one of the Rules of Golf's indelible moments – Ian Woosnam on the second tee at Royal Lytham & St. Annes with his hands on his hips and his eyes looking to the heavens for understanding while his caddie stands behind him with his head hung in disbelief and disappointment.

On the practice tee before the final round of the 2001 British Open, Woosnam was trying to decide which of two drivers he wanted to use that day. His testing apparently went a little longer than expected. His caddie and he hurried to the practice chipping and putting greens before moving to the first tee. As a contender, Woosnam's starting time was 2:15.

A design anomaly, the first hole at Lytham is a par 3. Woosnam struck a glorious 6-iron to within inches of the hole. In their haste to get underway and their focus toward the job at hand, Woosnam and his caddie had failed to count their clubs before starting. Both drivers that Woosnam had been testing on the practice ground were in his bag, 15 clubs in all, when he struck his first shot from the first tee. The fact that the first

27

hole is a par 3 may have added distraction. Had a driver been required, as is traditionally the case at an opening hole, the extra driver may have been discovered before play began.

The caddie discovered the violation on the first green and revealed it to his boss on the second tee. Instead of being tied for the lead in the British Open, Woosnam, following the two-stroke penalty [Rule 4-4], was now reeling in disbelief. He threw his hat to the ground and the extra club into the rough. "You've only got one job to think about and that's taking care of the bloody clubs," Woosnam was overheard to say to his caddie.

Although bogeying two of the next three holes, the Welshman's reconstitution was admirable. He eagled the sixth and played the last 13 in three under par. He finished tied for third, four shots behind David Duval.

In the press tent following the round, Woosnam was more forgiving of his caddie's mistake. "It is the biggest he will make in his life. He won't do it again. He's a good caddie…" And when asked if he has a system for counting his clubs, Woosnam replied, "Yeah. You start counting at one and stop when you get to 14."

Fourteen years before, in the 1987 Ryder Cup at Muirfield Village, Ben Crenshaw also suffered the consequences of Rule 4. In this instance, no penalty strokes were assessed. Walking down a gravel pathway, Crenshaw was lightly bouncing his putter along the ground in time with his steps when the club's shaft broke.

It did not matter that the damage was incurred without anger or malice. It was damaged "other than in the normal course of play" and, as such, could not be subsequently used or replaced during the round.

For the second nine holes, America's best putter used various clubs for putting – sometimes a 1-iron, sometimes a sand wedge. The Texan's misfortune, coupled with the intensity of the singles competition, seemed to provide extra focus and he continued to putt well. The match went to the 18th hole where Eamonn Darcy won 1 up.

With a final score of 15-13, the European Team won the Ryder Cup for the first time on American soil. Had Crenshaw won his match, the competition would have ended in a tie. Had that been the case, the Europeans, as defending champions, would still have retained the cup.

RULE **THE BALL**

DEFINITIONS

All defined terms are in *italics* and are listed alphabetically in the Definitions section – see pages 6–15.

5-1. GENERAL

The ball the player plays must conform to requirements specified in Appendix III.

Note: The *Committee* may require, in the conditions of a competition (Rule 33-1), that the ball the player plays must be named on the current List of Conforming Golf Balls issued by the United States Golf Association.

5-2. FOREIGN MATERIAL

Foreign material must not be applied to a ball for the purpose of changing its playing characteristics.

PENALTY FOR BREACH OF RULE 5-1 or 5-2:

Disqualification.

See **incident** involving Rule 5-3 on page 30

5-3. BALL UNFIT FOR PLAY

A ball is unfit for play if it is visibly cut, cracked or out of shape. A ball is not unfit for play solely because mud or other materials adhere to it, its surface is

scratched or scraped or its paint is damaged or discolored.

If a player has reason to believe his ball has become unfit for play during play of the hole being played, he may lift the ball without penalty to determine whether it is unfit.

Before lifting the ball, the player must announce his intention to his opponent in match play or his *marker* or a *fellow-competitor* in stroke play and mark the position of the ball.   He may then lift and examine it provided that he gives his opponent, *marker* or *fellow-competitor* an opportunity to examine the ball and observe the lifting and replacement. The ball must not be cleaned when lifted under Rule 5-3. If the player fails to comply with all or any part of this procedure, **he incurs a penalty of one stroke.**

If it is determined that the ball has become unfit for play during play of the hole being played, the player may *substitute* another ball, placing it on the spot where the original ball lay. Otherwise, the original ball must be replaced. If a player *substitutes* a ball when not permitted and he makes a *stroke* at the wrongly *substituted ball*, **he incurs the general penalty for a breach of Rule 5-3**, but there is no additional penalty under this Rule or Rule 15-1.

If a ball breaks into pieces as a result of a *stroke*, the *stroke* is cancelled and the player must play a ball without penalty as nearly as possible at the spot from which the original ball was played (see Rule 20-5).

*PENALTY FOR BREACH OF RULE 5-3:

Match play – Loss of hole; Stroke play – Two strokes.

*If a player incurs the general penalty for a breach of Rule 5-3, there is no additional penalty under this Rule.

Note: If the opponent, *marker* or *fellow-competitor* wishes to dispute a claim of unfitness, he must do so before the player plays another ball.

(Cleaning ball lifted from *putting green* or under any other *Rule* – see Rule 21)

RULE 5 INCIDENT

During the final match of the 1994 U.S. Amateur Championship, Tiger Woods learned that one of the very specific instances in the Rules when a referee is not to be involved, except as a last resort, is in determining whether or not a ball is unfit for play during the play of a hole.

One down to Trip Kuehne with five holes left in the 36-hole match, Woods' drive from the 14th tee of the TPC at Sawgrass struck a cart path and a media vehicle before finally coming to rest. The lie and angle to the green were good enough for him to reach the green with his second shot, which he did.

Once on the putting green, Woods marked and lifted his ball. It was then that he questioned whether or not his ball had been rendered unfit for play by virtue of its striking the path and the vehicle. Woods' inquiry was directed to the referee who was walking with the match. The referee responded that Woods would have to make that determination after giving his opponent an opportunity to examine the ball.

After inspecting Woods' ball, Kuehne said he was unsure whether or not it was unfit. This sent Woods back to the referee for an opinion.

While Decision 5-3/7 permits a referee to make such a call, it also states that every effort should be made to have the opponent, marker or fellow-competitor fulfill his responsibilities under Rule 5-3. In this situation, Woods' opponent was not able to fulfill his responsibilities because he did not know if a ball was unfit simply because it was scarred from bouncing off of a cart path.

With Kuehne unsure and Woods entitled to a ruling, the referee determined that a new ball could not be substituted. Rule 5-3 is specific in stating that a ball is not unfit when its surface is scratched or scraped or its paint is damaged or discolored.

Woods halved the hole with the scraped ball. After birdies at the 16th and 17th, Woods was 1 up. Woods' par, conceded by Kuehne at the 18th, gave Woods a 2 up victory and the first of his three consecutive U.S. Amateur titles.

RULE 6 — THE PLAYER

DEFINITIONS

All defined terms are in *italics* and are listed alphabetically in the Definitions section – see pages 6–15.

6-1. RULES
The player and his *caddie* are responsible for knowing the *Rules*. During a *stipulated round*, for any breach of a *Rule* by his *caddie*, the player incurs the applicable penalty.

6-2. HANDICAP
a. Match Play
Before starting a match in a handicap competition, the players should determine from one another their respective handicaps. If a player begins a match having declared a handicap higher than that to which he is entitled and this affects the number of strokes given or received, **he is disqualified**; otherwise, the player must play off the declared handicap.

b. Stroke Play
In any round of a handicap competition, the *competitor* must ensure that his handicap is recorded on his score card before it is returned to the *Committee*. If no handicap is recorded on his score card before it is returned (Rule 6-6b), or if the recorded handicap is higher than that to which he is entitled and this affects the number of strokes received, **he is disqualified** from the handicap competition; otherwise, the score stands.
Note: It is the player's responsibility to know the holes at which handicap strokes are to be given or received.

6-3. TIME OF STARTING AND GROUPS
a. Time of Starting
The player must start at the time established by the *Committee*.

b. Groups
In stroke play, the *competitor* must remain throughout the round in the

31

group arranged by the *Committee* unless the *Committee* authorizes or ratifies a change.

PENALTY FOR BREACH OF RULE 6-3:

Disqualification.

(*Best-ball* and *four-ball* play – see Rules 30-3a and 31-2)

Note: The *Committee* may provide in the conditions of a competition (Rule 33-1) that, if the player arrives at his starting point, ready to play, within five minutes after his starting time, in the absence of circumstances that warrant waiving the penalty of disqualification as provided in Rule 33-7, the penalty for failure to start on time is **loss of the first hole in match play or two strokes at the first hole in stroke play instead of disqualification.**

6-4. CADDIE

The player may be assisted by a *caddie*, but he is limited to only one *caddie* at any one time.

PENALTY FOR BREACH OF RULE 6-4:

Match play – At the conclusion of the hole at which the breach is discovered, the state of the match is adjusted by deducting one hole for each hole at which a breach occurred; maximum deduction per round – Two holes. Stroke play – Two strokes for each hole at which any breach occurred; maximum penalty per round – Four strokes. Match or stroke play – In the event of a breach between the play of two holes, the penalty applies to the next hole. A player having more than one *caddie* in breach of this Rule must immediately upon discovery that a breach has occurred ensure that he has no more than one *caddie* at any one time during the remainder of the *stipulated round*. Otherwise, the player is disqualified.

Bogey and par competitions – Penalties as in match play.

Stableford competitions – see Note 2 to Rule 32-1b

Note: The *Committee* may, in the conditions of a competition (Rule 33-1), prohibit the use of *caddies* or restrict a player in his choice of *caddie*.

6-5. BALL

The responsibility for playing the proper ball rests with the player. Each player should put an identification mark on his ball.

The responsibility for playing the proper ball rests with the player. PGA Tour player Duffy Waldorf has his wife and children assist him in putting identification marks on his golf balls.

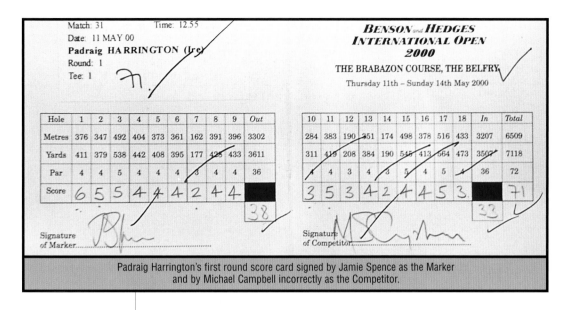

Padraig Harrington's first round score card signed by Jamie Spence as the Marker
and by Michael Campbell incorrectly as the Competitor.

6-6. SCORING IN STROKE PLAY
a. Recording Scores
After each hole the *marker* should check the score with the *competitor* and record it. On completion of the round the *marker* must sign the score card and hand it to the *competitor*. If more than one *marker* records the scores, each must sign for the part for which he is responsible.

b. Signing and Returning Score Card

See **incident** involving Rule 6-6b on page 37–38

After completion of the round, the *competitor* should check his score for each hole and settle any doubtful points with the *Committee*. He must ensure that the *marker* or *markers* have signed the score card, sign the score card himself and return it to the *Committee* as soon as possible.

PENALTY FOR BREACH OF RULE 6-6b:
Disqualification.

c. Alteration of Score Card
No alteration may be made on a score card after the *competitor* has returned it to the *Committee*.

d. Wrong Score for Hole

See **incident** involving Rule 6-6d on page 37–38

The *competitor* is responsible for the correctness of the score recorded for each hole on his score card. If he returns a score for any hole lower than actually taken, **he is disqualified**. If he returns a score for any hole higher than actually taken, the score as returned stands.
Note 1: The *Committee* is responsible for the addition of scores and application of the handicap recorded on the score card – see Rule 33-5.
Note 2: In *four-ball* stroke play, see also Rule 31-4 and -7a.

6-7. UNDUE DELAY; SLOW PLAY
The player must play without undue delay and in accordance with any pace of play guidelines that the *Committee* may establish. Between completion of a hole and playing from the next *teeing ground*, the player must not unduly delay play.

SCORING IN STROKE PLAY

COMPETITION SPRING STROKE PLAY   DATE 14 . 6 . 95

PLAYER D. BROWN   HANDICAP 10   Game No 21

Hole	Yards	Par	Stroke Index	Score	W=+ L=- H=0 POINTS	Mar Score	Hole	Yards	Par	Stroke Index	Score	W=+ L=- H=0 POINTS	Mar Score
1	312	4	17	5		6	10	369	4	12	6̶5 **c**		
2	446	4	1	4		4	11	433	4	2	3		
3	310	4	13	4		3	12	361	4	14	4		
4	370	4	9	5	**b**	5	13	415	4	6	5		
5	478	5	3	6			14	155	3	16	6		
8̶7	429	4	11	4			15	338	4	8	5		
7̶6	385	4	5	3			16	316	4	10	4		
8	178	3	7	4			17	191	3	4	5		
9	354	4	15	6			18	508	5	18	7		
OUT	3262			41			IN	3086	35		44		
							OUT	3262	36		41		
							TOTAL	6348	71		85		

a (against holes 6/7)

Markers Signature D.B. **e & f**

Players Signature Bill White

HANDICAP 10 **d**
NETT 75

Competitor's Responsibilities:

1. To record the correct handicap somewhere on the score card before it is returned to the Committee.
2. To check the gross score recorded for each hole is correct.
3. To ensure that the marker has signed the card and to countersign the card himself before it is returned to the Committee.

Committee Responsibilities:

1. Issue to each competitor a score card containing the date and the competitor's name.
2. To add the scores for each hole and apply the handicap recorded on the card.

(**a**) Hole numbers may be altered if hole scores have been recorded in the wrong boxes.
(**b**) A marker need not keep a record of his own score, however it is recommended.
(**c**) There is nothing in the Rules that requires an alteration to be initialled.
(**d**) The competitor is responsible only for the correctness of the score recorded for each hole. If the competitor records a wrong total score or net score, the Committee must correct the error, without penalty to the competitor. In this instance, the Committee have added the scores for each hole and applied the handicap.
(**e**) There is no penalty if a marker signs the competitor's score card in the space provided for the competitor's signature, and the competitor then signs in the space provided for the marker's signature.
(**f**) The initialing of the score card by the competitor is sufficient for the purpose of countersignature.

PENALTY FOR BREACH OF RULE 6-7:

Match play – Loss of hole

Stroke play – Two strokes

Bogey and par competitions – See Note 3 to Rule 32-1a.

Stableford competitions – See Note 3 to Rule 32-1b.

For subsequent offence – Disqualification.

Note 1: If the player unduly delays play between holes, he is delaying the play of the next hole and, except for bogey, par, and Stableford competitions (see Rule 32), the penalty applies to that hole.

Note 2: For the purpose of preventing slow play, the *Committee* may, in the conditions of a competition (Rule 33-1), establish pace of play guidelines including maximum periods of time allowed to complete a *stipulated round*, a hole or a *stroke*.

In stroke play only, the *Committee* may, in such a condition, modify the penalty for a breach of this Rule as follows:

First offence – One stroke. Second offence – Two strokes.

For subsequent offence – Disqualification.

6-8. DISCONTINUANCE OF PLAY; RESUMPTION OF PLAY
a. When Permitted

The player must not discontinue play unless:

(i)   the *Committee* has suspended play;

(ii)   he believes there is danger from lightning;

(iii)   he is seeking a decision from the *Committee* on a doubtful or disputed point (see Rules 2-5 and 34-3); or

(iv)   there is some other good reason such as sudden illness.

Bad weather is not of itself a good reason for discontinuing play.

If the player discontinues play without specific permission from the

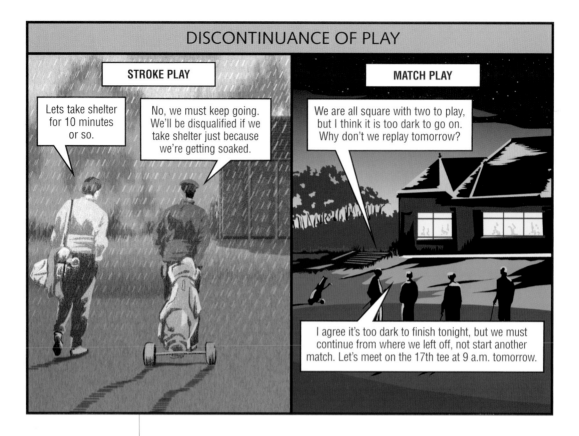

Committee, he must report to the Committee as soon as practicable. If he does so and the Committee considers his reason satisfactory, there is no penalty. Otherwise, **the player is disqualified**.

Exception in match play: Players discontinuing match play by agreement are not subject to disqualification unless by so doing the competition is delayed.

Note: Leaving the course does not of itself constitute discontinuance of play.

b. Procedure When Play Suspended by Committee

When play is suspended by the Committee, if the players in a match or group are between the play of two holes, they must not resume play until the Committee has ordered a resumption of play. If they have started play of a hole, they may discontinue play immediately or continue play of the hole, provided they do so without delay. If the players choose to continue play of the hole, they are permitted to discontinue play before completing it. In any case, play must be discontinued after the hole is completed.

The players must resume play when the Committee has ordered a resumption of play.

PENALTY FOR BREACH OF RULE 6-8b:

Disqualification.

Note: The Committee may provide in the conditions of a competition (Rule 33-1) that, in potentially dangerous situations, play must be discontinued immediately following a suspension of play by the Committee. If a player fails to discontinue play immediately, **he is disqualified** unless circumstances warrant waiving the penalty as provided in Rule 33-7.

c. Lifting Ball When Play Discontinued

When a player discontinues play of a hole under Rule 6-8a, he may lift his ball without penalty only if the *Committee* has suspended play or there is a good reason to lift it. Before lifting the ball the player must mark its position. If the player discontinues play and lifts his ball without specific permission from the *Committee*, he must, when reporting to the *Committee* (Rule 6-8a), report the lifting of the ball.

If the player lifts the ball without a good reason to do so, fails to mark the position of the ball before lifting it or fails to report the lifting of the ball, **he incurs a penalty of one stroke**.

d. Procedure When Play Resumed

Play must be resumed from where it was discontinued, even if resumption occurs on a subsequent day. The player must, either before or when play is resumed, proceed as follows:

(i)   If the player has lifted the ball, he must, provided he was entitled to lift it under Rule 6-8c, place a ball on the spot from which the original ball was lifted. Otherwise, the original ball must be placed on the spot from which it was lifted;

(ii)   If the player entitled to lift his ball under Rule 6-8c has not done so, he may lift, clean and replace the ball, or *substitute* a ball on the spot from which the original ball was lifted. Before lifting the ball he must mark its position; or

(iii)   If the player's ball or ball-marker is moved (including by wind or water) while play is discontinued, a ball or ball-marker must be placed on the spot from which the original ball or ball-marker was moved.

Note: If the spot where the ball is to be placed is impossible to determine, it must be estimated and the ball placed on the estimated spot. The provisions of Rule 20-3c do not apply.

*PENALTY FOR BREACH OF RULE 6-8c or d:

Match play – Loss of hole; Stroke play – Two strokes.

*If a player incurs the general penalty for a breach of Rule 6-8d, there is no additional penalty under Rule 6-8c.

RULE 6 INCIDENTS

The Rules of Golf are founded on the premise that the player bears ultimate responsibility for knowing and applying the rules and conditions under which the competition is to be played.

Starting at the time laid down by the Committee [Rule 6-3] is a criterion unalterable except in exceptional circumstances. Such an exception presented itself while the so-called Beltway Sniper was still at large during the first round of the 2002 Middle Atlantic Amateur Championship at Bethesda C.C. in Maryland.

A sniper shooting earlier in the day at a local school resulted in the lockdown of all schools in the area. Three entrants in the golf tournament were high school students who, because of the lockdown, were now prevented by events beyond their control from being at their starting point at the designated time.

After conferring with the players, their parents, the schools and the USGA, the Committee decided that the three players would be given until 3:40 that afternoon to begin play. The 54-hole competition could not be delayed beyond the first day. However, the 3:40 start would ensure that three students could finish before dark or, at the worst, have just a few holes to play the following morning. The lockdown was lifted at 3 p.m., and all three players were able to reach the golf course and play their first round.

As the ultimate testament to a player's performance in stroke play competition, the score card must never reflect a score lower than actually taken, must be signed by the competitor, attested by the marker and returned as soon as possible to the Committee.

Failure to meet any of these criteria results in disqualification. This is sometimes difficult for the golf world to accept when numerous, highly qualified Rules officials administer major championships and tour events.

At Royal St. George's, before beginning their third round play of the 2003 British Open, Mark Roe and Jesper Parnevik failed to exchange their cards on the first tee, which resulted in Roe recording Parnevik's scores on Roe's card, and visa versa. The hole scores were accurately recorded but attributed to the wrong player. Roe's brilliant 67, which included seven one putt greens, was recorded on Parnevik's card when, in fact, Parnevik had shot 81. Parnevik's 81 was submitted as Roe's score. The disqualifying errors were not discovered until both players had handed in their cards and left the scoring area.

While there was no question that Parnevik was disqualified, there was still a chance that the 81 he recorded on Roe's card might eek by, as it is not a violation of the Rules to submit a score higher than actually taken, only lower. Close comparison of the two cards, however, revealed that Parnevik had beaten Roe on one hole. Parnevik's birdie at the par-5 4th was one stroke lower than Roe had taken. Roe was, therefore, disqualified for submitting a score for a hole lower than actually taken. [Rule 6-6d; Decision 6-6d/4.]

"It's a mistake I've never made before," Roe reflected. "We obviously shook hands on the first tee and forgot to exchange score cards. Therefore, I wrote Jesper's scores on my card, and Jesper wrote my scores on his card. I bet he was happy with 67.

"I spent plenty of time in the [scoring] hut. I didn't rush in and rush out. Obviously, after having such a good day, I'm going to double and triple check my scores. I spent a lot of time. It's unfortunate that no one noticed, but there's no one else to blame but myself."

Roberto De Vicenzo signed for a higher score than he actually made at the 1968 Masters Tournament, which did not disqualify him, but did keep the Argentinean from forcing a playoff with Bob Goalby.

Playing in front of Goalby on Sunday, De Vicenzo, the reigning British Open Champion, sank a five-foot birdie put on the 17th hole for a 3. A bogey at the 18th gave him an 11-under-par total of 277. Goalby managed a five-footer for par at the 18th for a 66. His total was also 277.

However, De Vicenzo's fellow-competitor and marker, Tommy Aaron, had mistakenly recorded a 4 for De Vicenzo at the 17th, rather than the 3. In the hoopla of an anticipated playoff, De Vicenzo did not notice the mistake, signed and returned his card, and rushed away from the scorer's table to meet the press. A bit later, Aaron noticed the mistake and brought it to the attention of tournament officials.

Augusta National founder Bob Jones searched for a way around the error but none could be found. The Rules are clear. The higher score had to stand, and Bob Goalby was the Masters Champion. Like Roe 33 years later, De Vicenzo was generous in his understanding. "It's my fault. Tommy feels like I feel, very bad. I think the Rule is hard." The drama was compounded by the fact that it was De Vicenzo's 45th birthday.

In the excitement of Jackie Pung's apparent victory at the 1957 U.S. Women's Open, the Hawaiian signed for a correct final round total of 72, but included an incorrect hole score. At the 4th hole of Winged Foot's East Course, Pung's marker had recorded a five rather than her actual score of six.

A past U.S. Women's Amateur Champion and gallery favorite, Pung was told of her infraction shortly thereafter. Ironically, the victory fell to Betsy Rawls, who had won the 1953 Women's Open in a playoff with Pung. It was the third of Rawl's four U.S. Women's Open victories.

Failure to sign a first round score card cost Padraig Harrington the 2000 Benson and Hedges International Open at The Belfry. As he began warming up for the final round, holding a five-shot lead, the 28-year-old Irishman was informed by PGA European Tour officials that he was disqualified.

Members of the Committee began collecting Harrington's three previous score cards for souvenir purposes when it was discovered that he had not signed his first round card. Jamie Spence, his marker, had signed as required, but Michael Campbell, the third player in the group, had signed somehow instead of Harrington, who was disqualified. [Rule 6-6b.]

RULE **PRACTICE**

DEFINITIONS

All defined terms are in *italics* and are listed alphabetically in the Definitions section – see pages 6–15.

7-1. BEFORE OR BETWEEN ROUNDS
a. Match Play

On any day of a match play competition, a player may practice on the competition *course* before a round.

b. Stroke Play

Before a round or play-off on any day of a stroke play competition, a *competitor* must not practice on the competition *course* or test the surface of any *putting green* on the *course* by rolling a ball or roughening or scraping the surface.

When two or more rounds of a stroke play competition are to be played over consecutive days, a *competitor* must not practice between those rounds on any competition *course* remaining to be played, or test the surface of any *putting green* on such *course* by rolling a ball or roughening or scraping the surface.

Exception: Practice putting or chipping on or near the first *teeing ground* before starting a round or play-off is permitted.

PENALTY FOR BREACH OF RULE 7-1b:

Disqualification.

PRACTICE DURING A ROUND

Practice putting and chipping on or near the tee of the next hole to be played is permitted as long as play is not delayed.

Note: The *Committee* may, in the conditions of a competition (Rule 33-1), prohibit practice on the competition *course* on any day of a match play competition or permit practice on the competition *course* or part of the *course* (Rule 33-2c) on any day of or between rounds of a stroke play competition.

7-2. DURING ROUND

See **incident** involving Rule 7-2 on page 41

A player must not make a practice stroke during play of a hole.

Between the play of two holes a player must not make a practice *stroke*, except that he may practice putting or chipping on or near:

(i)   the *putting green* of the hole last played,

(ii)   any practice *putting green*, or

(iii)   the *teeing ground* of the next hole to be played in the round, provided a practice *stroke* is not made from a *hazard* and does not unduly delay play (Rule 6-7).

Strokes made in continuing the play of a hole, the result of which has been decided, are not practice *strokes*.

Exception: When play has been suspended by the *Committee*, a player may, prior to resumption of play, practice (a) as provided in this Rule, (b) anywhere other than on the competition *course* and (c) as otherwise permitted by the *Committee*.

PENALTY FOR BREACH OF RULE 7-2:

Match play – Loss of hole; Stroke play – Two strokes.

In the event of a breach between the play of two holes, the penalty applies to the next hole.

Note 1: A practice swing is not a practice *stroke* and may be taken at any place, provided the player does not breach the *Rules*.

Note 2: The *Committee* may, in the conditions of a competition (Rule 33-1), prohibit:

(a)   practice on or near the *putting green* of the hole last played, and

(b)   rolling a ball on the *putting green* of the hole last played.

RULE 7 INCIDENT

Vickie Odegard was penalized two strokes at the 2000 U.S. Women's Open when she dropped several balls on the back tee at the 5th hole and practiced her putting.

Under Rule 7-2, as long as it does not cause a delay, practice putting and chipping is permitted on the putting green of the last hole played or the teeing ground of the next hole to be played.

The problem was that Odegard practiced on a back tee — an area mowed as a tee — and that area was approximately 30 yards from the 5th hole's teeing ground. By definition, the teeing ground is a rectangular area two club-lengths in depth, the front and sides of which are defined by the outside limits of the two tee-markers. On the back tee, Odegard was not considered on or near the next teeing ground.

Because the infraction took place between holes, the two-stroke penalty was applied to the next hole, the 5th hole.

At the 1993 U.S. Open at Baltusrol Golf Club, during a period of slow play, Tom Watson took advantage of this Rule to practice his putting and change the momentum of his game that day. Watson's group finished play of the 5th hole and then found it necessary to wait before playing from the 6th tee. Concurrently, the group behind Watson's group had dropped far enough back so they were not in a position to play to the 5th green.

Cognizant of Rule 7-2, Watson confirmed that it was permissible for him to hit some practice putts as long as he wasn't delaying play. He then dropped a couple of balls on the green and holed some rather long putts. The confidence gained from this practice was apparently valuable because over the ensuing holes, Watson made more than one sizeable putt for birdie.

Also under Rule 7-2, the Committee may permit practice on the course after play has been suspended and prior to resumption. Thick fog forced a suspension of play during the first round of the 2000 U.S. Open at Pebble Beach. Because it was not a dangerous situation and because the Committee sanctioned it, those players who were between holes were permitted to practice under the stipulations of Rule 7-2.

When it was evident that the fog would not clear quickly, the players were evacuated from the course and returned to the clubhouse. When the first round resumed the following morning, Rule 7-2 was also applicable before the siren announced the resumption of play.

RULE | ## ADVICE; INDICATING LINE OF PLAY

DEFINITIONS | All defined terms are in *italics* and are listed alphabetically in the Definitions section – see pages 6–15.

See **incident** involving Rule 8-1 on page 44

8-1. ADVICE

During a *stipulated round*, a player must not:

(a) give *advice* to anyone in the competition playing on the *course* other

41

than his *partner*, or

(b) ask for *advice* from anyone other than his *partner* or either of their *caddies*.

8-2. INDICATING LINE OF PLAY
a. Other Than on Putting Green
Except on the *putting green*, a player may have the *line of play* indicated to him by anyone, but no one may be positioned by the player on or close to the line or an extension of the line beyond the *hole* while the *stroke* is being made. Any mark placed by the player or with his knowledge to indicate the line must be removed before the *stroke* is made.

Exception: *Flagstick* attended or held up – see Rule 17-1.

b. On the Putting Green

See **incident** involving Rule 8-2b on page 43–4

When the player's ball is on the *putting green*, the player, his *partner* or either of their *caddies* may, before but not during the *stroke*, point out a line for putting, but in so doing the *putting green* must not be touched. A mark must not be placed anywhere to indicate a line for putting.

PENALTY FOR BREACH OF RULE:
Match play – Loss of hole; Stroke play – Two strokes.

Note: The *Committee* may, in the conditions of a team competition (Rule 33-1), permit each team to appoint one person who may give *advice* (including pointing out a line for putting) to members of that team. The *Committee* may establish conditions relating to the appointment and permitted conduct of that person, who must be identified to the *Committee* before giving *advice*.

RULE 8 INCIDENTS

During the third round of the 1991 PGA Championship while advising John Daly about the break of a putt on Crooked Stick's 11th green, Daly's caddie, Jeff "Squeeky" Medlen, accidentally touched the green with the flagstick.

As ninth alternate, Daly had been included in the championship field when Nick Price withdrew to be present for the birth of his child, and three alternates ahead of Daly declined for various reasons. The unknown Arkansan had taken the outright lead for the title after posting a 69 and 67 for the first and second rounds respectively. Playing with Bruce Lietzke on Saturday, Daly was on his way to a third round 69. At the 11th, Medlen used his hand to point out the line of Daly's first putt. In his other hand, Medlen held the flagstick and inadvertently allowed it to touch the green.

The potential infraction was televised to millions and, fortunately, videotaped for review. Alerted almost immediately to what had taken place, PGA of America Rules officials met Daly at the end of the round to discuss the matter and make a decision about a possible infraction before Daly returned his score card.

Daly, Medlen, Lietzke and Rules officials climbed into courtesy cars and rode to a television trailer to view the videotape. The tape showed Medlen holding the removed flagstick and allowing it to touch the putting green about three feet to the right of the hole while indicating the line of putt with his other hand. Rule 8-2 states that, while a line for putting may be pointed out, the green shall not be touched in doing so.

After speaking with all involved and watching the tape, the referee was convinced that Daly's left-to-right breaking putt was never in danger of reaching the spot where the flagstick had touched the green and that no mark had been left to aid Daly with the putt. Daly missed that putt, and the resulting tap-in was also unaffected by the flagstick having touched the green. No penalty was incurred. Daly returned his third round card with a score of 69. The following day, he won the PGA Championship by three shots.

On the 17th hole at Long Cove Club during the stroke play qualifying rounds of the 1991 U.S. Mid-Amateur Championship, David Eger offered his fellow-competitor a suggestion with regard to the Rules. The well-intended remark was nevertheless rewarded with a two-stroke penalty.

Previous to the remark, Eger had played his tee shot onto the putting green. The second player's tee shot had erred so far into the scrub and trees on the left that he played a provisional ball, which finished on the putting green.

As the second player went into the scrub to search for his first ball, Eger suggested it might be wiser to leave the first ball unfound and play the second ball that was already on the green in three strokes.

Information on the Rules is not advice. However, Decision 8-1/16 states that a suggestion that could influence another player "in determining his play" is advice. A Rules official overheard Eger's comment and a penalty of two strokes was assessed.

RULE

INFORMATION AS TO STROKES TAKEN

DEFINITIONS

All defined terms are in *italics* and are listed alphabetically in the Definitions section – see pages 6–15.

9-1. GENERAL
The number of *strokes* a player has taken includes any *penalty strokes* incurred.

9-2. MATCH PLAY
a. Information as to Strokes Taken
An opponent is entitled to ascertain from the player, during the play of a hole, the number of *strokes* he has taken and, after play of a hole, the number of *strokes* taken on the hole just completed.

See **incident** involving Rule 9-2 on page 45–46

b. Wrong Information
A player must not give wrong information to his opponent. If a player gives wrong information, **he loses the hole.**

A player is deemed to have given wrong information if he:
(i)   fails to inform his opponent as soon as practicable that he has incurred a penalty, unless (a) he was obviously proceeding under a *Rule* involving a penalty and this was observed by his opponent; or (b) he corrects the mistake before his opponent makes his next stroke; or
(ii)   gives incorrect information during play of a hole regarding the number of *strokes* taken and does not correct the mistake before his opponent makes his next *stroke*; or

INFORMATION AS TO STROKES TAKEN

Just before you play, I had to declare my ball unplayable in there, so I've now played three.

O.K. Thanks for letting me know.

(iii) gives incorrect information regarding the number of *strokes* taken to complete a hole and this affects the opponent's understanding of the result of the hole, unless he corrects the mistake before any player makes a *stroke* from the next *teeing ground* or, in the case of the last hole of the match, before all players leave the *putting green*.

A player has given wrong information even if it is due to the failure to include a penalty that he did not know he had incurred. It is the player's responsibility to know the *Rules*.

9-3. STROKE PLAY
A *competitor* who has incurred a penalty should inform his *marker* as soon as practicable.

RULE 9 INCIDENT

On the 7th tee of Kiawah Island's Ocean Course during the first morning's foursomes of the 1991 Ryder Cup Matches, Chip Beck and Paul Azinger were overheard by their European opponents discussing which type of ball they would use to optimize their performance during the play of that hole.

The Americans mistakenly believed that because one of them played a 90-compression ball and the other a 100-compression ball, they were entitled to a choice as to which they could use.

A version of the so-called One-Ball Rule from the Rules of Golf's Appendix I was in effect and stipulated that a player must use the same brand and type of ball for the entire round. Whichever player's turn it was to drive was required to use the type of ball with which that player had begun the round. An option was not created just because his partner was using a different type of ball. With one player driving the odd-numbered holes and the other driving the even-numbered holes, as required during foursome competition, the Americans were mistaken in thinking they had a choice of ball types.

Unknowingly and mistakenly, the Americans made the choice and the wrong type of ball was played from the tee. The European side of Seve Ballesteros and Jose Maria Olazabal suspected this was a breach of the Rules. Sam Torrance, a European team member who was not playing in the first morning's matches, was in the gallery and following the match. He was motioned over by Ballesteros, told of the situation and sent to fetch the European Captain Bernard Gallacher.

While Gallacher was being located, play of the 7th, 8th and 9th holes was completed. On the way to the 10th tee, the Europeans made a claim concerning what had taken place at the 7th hole. The chief referee was called to settle the dispute.

In match play, Rule 9-2 requires a player who has incurred a penalty to notify his opponent as soon as practicable. If he does not, even when he doesn't know he has incurred a penalty, he is considered to have given wrong information. In this case, the American side gave wrong information as a penalty was associated with their playing of the wrong type of ball from the 7th tee. However, since the European side was aware of the error and did not make a claim (Rule 2-5) before anyone played from the 8th tee, their belated claim could not be considered. It was as if the statute of limitations had run out for that particular violation.

The match continued from the 10th tee without Beck and Azinger being penalized for their infraction at the 7th hole.

RULE 10

ORDER OF PLAY

DEFINITIONS

All defined terms are in *italics* and are listed alphabetically in the Definitions section – see pages 6–15.

10-1. MATCH PLAY
a. When Starting Play of Hole
The *side* that has the *honor* at the first *teeing ground* is determined by the order of the draw. In the absence of a draw, the *honor* should be decided by lot.

The *side* that wins a hole takes the *honor* at the next *teeing ground*. If a hole has been halved, the *side* that had the *honor* at the previous *teeing ground* retains it.

b. During Play of Hole

See **incident** involving Rule 10-1b on page 48

After both players have started play of the hole, the ball farther from the *hole* is played first. If the balls are equidistant from the *hole* or their positions relative to the *hole* are not determinable, the ball to be played first should be decided by lot.
Exception: Rule 30-3c (*best-ball* and *four-ball* match play).
Note: When the original ball is not to be played as it lies and the player is required to play a ball as nearly as possible at the spot from which the original ball was last played (see Rule 20-5), the order of play is determined by the spot from which the previous *stroke* was made. When a ball may be played from a spot other than where the previous *stroke* was made, the order of play is

determined by the position where the original ball came to rest.

c. Playing Out of Turn

If a player plays when his opponent should have played, there is no penalty, but the opponent may immediately require the player to cancel the *stroke* so made and, in correct order, play a ball as nearly as possible at the spot from which the original ball was last played (see Rule 20-5).

10-2. STROKE PLAY
a. When Starting Play of Hole

The *competitor* who has the *honor* at the first *teeing ground* is determined by the order of the draw. In the absence of a draw, the *honor* should be decided by lot.

The *competitor* with the lowest score at a hole takes the *honor* at the next *teeing ground*. The *competitor* with the second lowest score plays next and so on. If two or more *competitors* have the same score at a hole, they play from the next *teeing ground* in the same order as at the previous *teeing ground*.

b. During Play of Hole

After the *competitors* have started play of the hole, the ball farthest from the *hole* is played first. If two or more balls are equidistant from the *hole* or their positions relative to the *hole* are not determinable, the ball to be played first should be decided by lot.

Exceptions: Rules 22 (ball assisting or interfering with play) and 31-5 (*four-ball* stroke play).

Note: When the original ball is not to be played as it lies and the player is required to play a ball as nearly as possible at the spot from which the original ball was last played (see Rule 20-5), the order of play is determined by the spot from which the previous *stroke* was made. When a ball may be played from a spot other than where the previous *stroke* was made, the order of play is determined by the position where the original ball came to rest.

c. Playing Out of Turn

If a *competitor* plays out of turn, there is no penalty and the ball is played as it lies. If, however, the *Committee* determines that *competitors* have agreed to play out of turn to give one of them an advantage, **they are disqualified**. (Making stroke while another ball in motion after stroke from putting green – see Rule 16-1f.)

(Incorrect order of play in *threesomes* and *foursomes* stroke play – see Rule 29-3.)

10-3. PROVISIONAL BALL OR SECOND BALL FROM TEEING GROUND

If a player plays a *provisional ball* or a second ball from a *teeing ground*, he must do so after his opponent or *fellow-competitor* has played his first *stroke*. If a player plays a *provisional ball* or a second ball out of turn, Rule 10-1c or -2c applies.

RULE 10 INCIDENT

Phil Mickelson had the honor on the 17th tee, the third playoff hole, of the 2001 Buick Invitational at Torrey Pines' South Course. An extraordinary series of events ultimately gave Frank Lickliter the obligation to play first when both players returned to the tee a short time later.

Both men played their drives into a deep, ragged canyon left of the fairway drive zone. In the same order of play, [Rule 10-3] each then played a provisional ball in case their original ball was lost in the canyon.

Lickliter's ball was soon found requiring him to abandon his provisional ball in the fairway. [Rule 27-2c.] He determined that his ball was unplayable and chose to replay from the tee, as was his first option under the unplayable ball rule. [Rule 28a.]

In an unusual circumstance [see Rule 27 Incident on page 121], Mickelson ultimately found himself in the same situation as Lickliter.

Both players' drives were found, both players' provisional balls had to be abandoned, and both decided to return to the tee to play their third strokes.

Because play of the hole was still underway, the honor was no longer an issue. By definition, the honor is given to the first player to play from the tee. Mickelson had the honor when play of the hole began, but with play underway, the order of play is always determined by the relative position of the golf balls in question before relief from any situation is taken. [Rule 10-2b.]

In the canyon, before they were declared unplayable, Lickliter's ball lay farther from the hole than Mickelson's. Thus, it was Lickliter's turn to play. This point was obfuscated by the fact that both players' decision to take relief from an unplayable situation returned them to the same place from which they had played their previous stroke, the tee. On its face, it appeared they were restarting play of the 17th hole when, in fact, they were continuing play of the hole.

Rules officials correctly directed the players. Lickliter played first and his third shot found the fairway. Mickelson played next and his ball struck a tree on the left and dropped into the rough. Mickelson, the defending champion, ultimately won with a double bogey six.

RULE **11** | **TEEING GROUND**

DEFINITIONS

All defined terms are in *italics* and are listed alphabetically in the Definitions section – see pages 6–15.

11-1. TEEING

When the player's ball is to be teed within the *teeing ground*, it must be placed on:
- the surface of the *teeing ground*, including an irregularity of surface (whether or not created by the player), or
- a *tee* placed in or on the surface of the *teeing ground*, or
- sand or other natural substance placed on the surface of the *teeing ground*.

A player may stand outside the *teeing ground* to play a ball within it.

In teeing, if a player uses a non-conforming *tee* or any other object to raise the ball off the ground, **he is disqualified**.

11-2. TEE-MARKERS

Before a player makes his first *stroke* with any ball on the *teeing ground* of the hole being played, the tee-markers are deemed to be fixed. In these circumstances, if the player moves or allows to be moved a tee-marker for the purpose of avoiding interference with his *stance*, the area of his intended swing or his *line of play*, **he incurs the penalty for a breach of Rule 13-2.**

11-3. BALL FALLING OFF TEE

If a ball, when not *in play*, falls off a *tee* or is knocked off a *tee* by the player in *addressing* it, it may be re-teed without penalty. However, if a *stroke* is made at the ball in these circumstances, whether the ball is moving or not, the *stroke* counts but there is no penalty.

11-4. PLAYING FROM OUTSIDE TEEING GROUND
a. Match Play

If a player, when starting a hole, plays a ball from outside the *teeing ground* there is no penalty, but the opponent may immediately require the player to cancel the *stroke* and play a ball from within the *teeing ground*.

b. Stroke Play

See **incident** involving Rule 11-4b on page 50

If a *competitor*, when starting a hole, plays a ball from outside the *teeing ground*, **he incurs a penalty of two strokes** and must then play a ball from within the *teeing ground*.

If the *competitor* plays a *stroke* from the next *teeing ground* without first correcting his mistake or, in the case of the last hole of the round, leaves the *putting green* without first declaring his intention to correct his mistake, **he is disqualified.**

The *stroke* from outside the *teeing ground* and any subsequent *strokes* by the *competitor* on the hole prior to his correction of the mistake do not count in his score.

11-5. PLAYING FROM WRONG TEEING GROUND

The provisions of Rule 11-4 apply.

RULE 11 INCIDENT

The result of the 1990 U.S. Open Championship lent substantiation to the USGA's 18-hole playoff policy. A tie at eight-under-par, 280, joined Mike Donald and Hale Irwin after 72 holes of regulation play.

It would take another full trip around Medinah's No. 3 course and, even then, it would not be decided.

However, a momentary lapse of concentration regarding the Rules of Golf might have determined the winner had it not been for the diligence of the attending referee.

"After a long week, I was tired" said C. Grant Spaeth, former USGA president and the official accompanying the playoff. "Walking off the 17th green, I was tempted not to go down a hill to the 18th tee, which sits out on a peninsula that stretches into the lake.

"I thought I might cut over to the 18th fairway, contrary to the strictures in the book (the USGA manual that suggests walking Rules officials and referees be present at each teeing ground.) Thank God I resisted and trudged back to the tee."

The drama and competitive tension at Medinah Country Club had been intense all week. Irwin, 45, had summoned a wave of talent reflective of his 33 professional victories, which included two previous U.S. Open victories in 1974 and 1979. Indeed, he had holed a 45-foot birdie putt on the 72nd hole of regulation play to force the Monday playoff. Donald, 34, was the journeyman hopeful whose only PGA Tour victory had come the previous year in Williamsburg, VA.

After hours of athletic and psychological endurance, the players walked off the 17th green of the playoff round with Donald leading by one. As is sometimes the case in the waning moments of a long, intense contest, fatigue and lack of focus are cause for mistakes and lack of judgment. So it was on the 18th tee.

"If you look carefully at the films," Spaeth continues, "you will note that Mike Donald actually teed up in front of the markers, which I caught, whereupon he re-teed the ball. What an awful ending that could have been."

Rule 11, as it applies to stroke play, is exact. If a competitor plays from outside the teeing ground, he shall incur a penalty of two strokes and shall then play a ball from within the teeing ground. Had Donald's mistake been observed a few moments later, after he had played from ahead of the markers, the resulting two-stroke penalty would have given Irwin an almost insurmountable lead and the victory.

Spaeth's correction prevented the infraction, but Donald's bogey at the 90th hole resulted in both men scoring 74 in the playoff round. By the terms and conditions outlined in the entry form, and for the first time in its history, the U.S. Open then moved to sudden death to determine the winner.

On the first sudden death hole, the 91st hole of the championship, Irwin holed an eight-foot birdie putt to become the U.S. Open's oldest winner.

RULE **12** SEARCHING FOR AND IDENTIFYING BALL

DEFINITIONS All defined terms are in *italics* and are listed alphabetically in the Definitions section – see pages 6–15.

12-1. SEARCHING FOR BALL; SEEING BALL

In searching for his ball anywhere on the *course*, the player may touch or bend long grass, rushes, bushes, whins, heather or the like, but only to the extent necessary to find and identify it, provided that this does not improve the lie of the ball, the area of his intended *stance* or swing or his *line of play*.

A player is not necessarily entitled to see his ball when playing a *stroke*.

In a *hazard*, if a ball is believed to be covered by *loose impediments* or sand, the player may remove by probing or raking with a club or otherwise, as many *loose impediments* or as much sand as will enable him to see a part of the ball. If an excess is removed, there is no penalty and the ball must be re-covered so that only a part of it is visible. If the ball is *moved* during the removal, there is no penalty; the ball must be replaced and, if necessary, re-covered. As to removal of *loose impediments* outside a *hazard*, see Rule 23.

51

If a ball lying in an *abnormal ground condition* is accidentally *moved* during search, there is no penalty; the ball must be replaced, unless the player elects to proceed under Rule 25-1b. If the player replaces the ball, he may still proceed under Rule 25-1b if applicable.

If a ball is believed to be lying in water in a *water hazard*, the player may probe for it with a club or otherwise. If the ball is *moved* in probing, it must be replaced, unless the player elects to proceed under Rule 26-1. There is no penalty for causing the ball to *move* provided the movement of the ball was directly attributable to the specific act of probing. Otherwise, **the player incurs a *penalty stroke* under Rule 18-2a.**

PENALTY FOR BREACH OF RULE 12-1:

Match play – loss of hole; Stroke play – Two strokes.

12-2. IDENTIFYING BALL

See **incident** involving Rule 12-2 on page 53

The responsibility for playing the proper ball rests with the player. Each player should put an identification mark on his ball.

Except in a *hazard*, if a player has reason to believe a ball is his, he may lift the ball without penalty to identify it.

Before lifting the ball, the player must announce his intention to his opponent in match play or his *marker* or a *fellow-competitor* in stroke play and mark the position of the ball. He may then lift the ball and identify it provided that he gives his opponent, *marker* or *fellow-competitor* an opportunity to observe the lifting and replacement. The ball must not be cleaned beyond the extent necessary for identification when lifted under Rule 12-2. If the player fails to comply with all or any part of this procedure, or he lifts his ball for identification in a *hazard*, **he incurs a penalty of one stroke.**

If the lifted ball is the player's ball he must replace it. If he fails to do so, **he incurs the general penalty for a breach of Rule 12-2**, but there is no additional penalty under this Rule.

*PENALTY FOR BREACH OF RULE 12-2

Match play – Loss of hole; Stroke play – Two strokes.

*If a player incurs the general penalty for a breach of Rule 12-2, there is no additional penalty under this Rule.

SEARCHING FOR BALL IN BUNKER

If a player's ball is buried in a bunker, he may search for it by probing the sand with his fingers or he may use a rake. If the ball is moved, there is no penalty, but it must be replaced and, if necessary, re-covered so that only part of it is visible.

RULE 12 INCIDENT

The extraordinary events that surround televised golf competitions are sometimes to blame for creating bizarre Rules situations, and are sometimes to be credited with resolving them.

Having just completed his assignment during the third round of the 2001 World Golf Championships-NEC Invitational, John Paramor, chief referee for the European PGA Tour, was enjoying a quiet moment in one of the office trailers that was onsite to provide temporary, administrative space at Firestone C.C.

Simultaneously, Phil Mickelson was teeing his ball at the 16th hole and subsequently drove it into the right rough near a brick wall. Suggested, but not required under the Rules [Rule 12-2], Mickelson had atypically failed to put an identifying mark on his ball before playing from the tee. Once found, the lack of such a mark made positive identification less than certain in Mickelson's mind, and he was hesitant to assume the ball was his without such positive identification.

In the trailer, Paramor was watching the situation on television. "There was some great camera work from the blimp overhead," Paramor recalls. "[Phil's] ball was always in vision from the moment he struck it. You could pinpoint within a square foot where the ball had landed."

Paramor radioed his colleague to say that the blimp pictures were precise. "I told him that [according to the television footage] the ball should be so many yards to the right of the wall and so many yards in front of the shadow from a nearby tree. It was possible to get within a square foot of where the ball landed." The location Paramor described was exactly where a ball, only one, of the type Mickelson was playing had been found.

In this curious situation, talented camera work made positive identification possible, and compensated for the lack of an identifying mark on Mickelson's ball.

However, there was "a sting in the tail," as Paramor puts it. In the distraction of events surrounding identification of the ball, Mickelson lifted his ball for identification purposes without first notifying his fellow-competitor that he intended to do so. The result was a one stroke penalty. [Rule 12-2.]

RULE

BALL PLAYED AS IT LIES

DEFINITIONS

All defined terms are in *italics* and are listed alphabetically in the Definitions section – see pages 6–15.

13-1. GENERAL

The ball must be played as it lies, except as otherwise provided in the *Rules*.
(Ball at rest moved – see Rule 18)

IMPROVING AREA OF INTENDED SWING OR LINE OF PLAY

A player must not break an interfering branch or remove sand which is off the putting green but on the line of play.

See **incident** involving Rule 13-2 on page 57–58

13-2. IMPROVING LIE, AREA OF INTENDED STANCE OR SWING, OR LINE OF PLAY

A player must not improve or allow to be improved:

- the position or lie of his ball,
- the area of his intended *stance* or swing,
- his *line of play* or a reasonable extension of that line beyond the *hole*, or
- the area in which he is to drop or place a ball,

by any of the following actions:

- moving, bending or breaking anything growing or fixed (including immovable *obstructions* and objects defining *out of bounds*),

CREATING OR ELIMINATING IRREGULARITIES OF SURFACE

May I replace this divot in its hole which is on my line of play?

I am afraid you can't do that as you would be improving your line of play by eliminating an irregularity of surface.

IMPROVING AREA OF INTENDED STANCE

- creating or eliminating irregularities of surface,
- removing or pressing down sand, loose soil, replaced divots or other cut turf placed in position, or
- removing dew, frost or water.

However, the player incurs no penalty if the action occurs:

- in fairly taking his *stance*,
- in making a *stroke* or the backward movement of his club for a *stroke* and the *stroke* is made,
- on the *teeing ground* in creating or eliminating irregularities of surface (Rule 11-1), or

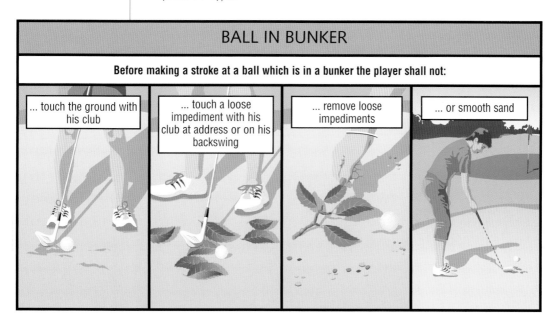

- on the *putting green* in removing sand and loose soil or in repairing damage (Rule 16-1).

The club may be grounded only lightly and must not be pressed on the ground.

Exception: Ball in *hazard* – see Rule 13-4.

13-3. BUILDING STANCE

A player is entitled to place his feet firmly in taking his *stance*, but he must not build a *stance*.

13-4. BALL IN HAZARD; PROHIBITED ACTIONS

See **incident** involving Rule 13-4 below

Except as provided in the *Rules*, before making a *stroke* at a ball that is in a *hazard* (whether a *bunker* or a *water hazard*) or that, having been lifted from a *hazard*, may be dropped or placed in the *hazard*, the player must not:

a. Test the condition of the *hazard* or any similar *hazard*;

b. Touch the ground in the *hazard* or water in the *water hazard* with his hand or a club; or

c. Touch or move a *loose impediment* lying in or touching the *hazard*.

Exceptions:

1. Provided nothing is done that constitutes testing the condition of the *hazard* or improves the lie of the ball, there is no penalty if the player (a) touches the ground in any *hazard* or water in a *water hazard* as a result of or to prevent falling, in removing an *obstruction*, in measuring or in retrieving, lifting, placing or replacing a ball under any *Rule* or (b) places his clubs in a *hazard*.

2. After making the *stroke*, the player or his *caddie* may smooth sand or soil in the *hazard*, provided that, if the ball is still in the *hazard* or has been lifted from the *hazard* and may be dropped or placed in the *hazard*, nothing is done that improves the lie of the ball or assists the player in his play.

Note: At any time, including at *address* or in the backward movement for the *stroke*, the player may touch with a club or otherwise any *obstruction*, any construction declared by the *Committee* to be an integral part of the *course* or any grass, bush, tree or other growing thing.

PENALTY FOR BREACH OF RULE:

Match play – Loss of hole; Stroke play – Two strokes.

(Searching for ball – see Rule 12-1)

(Relief for ball in *water hazard* – see Rule 26)

RULE 13 INCIDENTS

There are logical consistencies within the Rules of Golf, although they are sometimes difficult to discern. For example, under Rule 23, a loose impediment must be loose. A blade of grass stuck to a ball is not loose even though you could remove it easily, but a large boulder sitting on the desert floor is loose even though you would need a number of people to help you move it. Under Rule 18, the penalty is the same whether you kicked your ball or a coin simply fell from your hand, causing the ball to move, as you leaned over to mark your ball.

Under Rule 13, the tenet of playing the ball as it lies is protected in this same way from the most obvious violation, as well as the seemingly minor. The principals encased in the Rules are the same regardless of the magnitude of circumstances in which they are brought to bear.

Obvious to all was Thomas Bjorn's costly error at the 2003 British Open. Two-under par on the tee of the 17th hole during the first round, the Dane played his third to a greenside bunker. The fluffy bunker sand at Royal St. George's befuddled Bjorn, and he left his first attempt at extraction in the bunker. "I don't think I left a ball in a bunker for about ten years," Bjorn told reporters later. "And I know what I do every time I hit a bad bunker shot, lots of players do that as well, you just kind of check the sand … I dropped the club down in the sand to check … Unfortunately, in that situation, I wasn't out of the bunker [a two-stroke penalty under Rule 13-4], and I was probably not thinking clearly at the time.

"I was playing some of the best golf of my life. I was two-under, in those conditions, standing on the 17th tee, and then all of a sudden I was looking at a double bogey, at the best [without the penalty], and it turned into a quad … I walked over to the referee and said this is what I've done, I'll take my two-shot penalty."

The final result of the championship left Bjorn one shot away from tying for the lead and forcing a playoff with Ben Curtis, the Champion Golfer for 2003.

Larry Nelson used his understanding of Rule 13-4 to his advantage in an unusual situation at the 2001 Tradition. Nelson's second came to rest on a wooden bridge spanning a greenside water hazard at the par-5 15th. The area of his intended swing was unencumbered and the ball was playable on the decking in the open part of the bridge. Under the Note to Rule 13-4, a player is permitted to touch, with a club or otherwise, any obstruction in a hazard.

After confirming his rights with a Rules Official [Decision 13-4/30], Nelson went to a different portion of the bridge, practiced a few swings to get the feel of his club on the planking, and then pitched his ball to within 12 feet of the hole. During this process, Nelson had to be careful not to cause his ball to move [Rule 18] or to move any loose impediments in the hazard that may have been lying on the bridge [Rule 23].

The basic prohibition against improving your lie, stance, swing or line of play is addressed under the second section of Rule 13. Duffy Waldorf discovered that, no matter how innocuous the violation, the penalty is two strokes. At the 2003 FBR Capital Open in suburban Washington, D.C., Waldorf was playing this second shot to the 12th hole during the final round, which was being played on Monday due to previously inclement weather.

Waldorf addressed his ball and then stepped away after being distracted by something in the background. Regrouping before restarting his setup routine, he stepped forward, reached ahead with his club and tapped down some sort of irregularity or pitch mark in front of his ball. Rule 13 prohibits the improvement of the line of play. The line of play is defined as the direction the player wishes his ball to take after a stroke, plus "a reasonable distance on either side of the intended direction."

The Committee was faced with judging whether the irregularity that Waldorf tapped down was on his line of play. The hole that day was cut on the right side of the 12th green and Waldorf intended to play a cut shot. After reviewing videotape of the incident over and over again in the television compound, the Committee decided that the irregularity was within a reasonable distance of Waldorf's line of play, and two penalty strokes were assessed. In this particular incident, the player's action did not improve the stroke he played or his immediate lie. It was, however, an improvement to the line, a violation of the Rules and the penalty had to be assessed.

Scott Hoch found himself in an indisputable violation of the same Rule three years earlier at The Memorial. At Muirfield Village's par-4 10th hole, Hoch found his ball under several branches of a large evergreen tree. There was room for Hoch to play from under the tree, but one particularly low hanging branch interfered directly with his backswing. No Rules officials were nearby, but a television cameraman was and recorded the entire episode.

Understandably irritated by the interfering branch, Hoch several times retook his stance and practiced his takeaway in order to find the best way to hold the interfering branch out of the way of his intended swing. A player is allowed to fairly take his stance, but is prohibited from moving, bending or breaking anything growing or fixed that might improve the area of his intended stance or swing. [Rule 13-2.]

Adverbs raise interpretive questions in the Rules. "Fairly taking his stance" is described in detail in Decision 13-2/1. If backing into a branch or bending it are the only ways to take a stance for the stroke, this is permitted. Deliberately moving, bending or breaking branches in order to get them out of the way for the shot is not permitted. Hoch pushed the interfering branch out of his way by backing into it on his way to taking his stance when his stance could have been taken without bending the branch. This is clear from the television footage. Hoch was offered, but declined, a viewing of the tape and accepted the Rules Official's decision. Two penalty strokes were assessed.

RULE  STRIKING THE BALL

DEFINITIONS | All defined terms are in *italics* and are listed alphabetically in the Definitions section – see pages 6–15.

14-1. BALL TO BE FAIRLY STRUCK AT
The ball must be fairly struck at with the head of the club and must not be pushed, scraped or spooned.

14-2. ASSISTANCE
In making a *stroke*, a player must not:
a. accept physical assistance or protection from the elements; or
b. allow his *caddie*, his *partner* or his *partner's caddie* to position himself on or close to an extension of the *line of play* or the *line of putt* behind the ball.

PENALTY FOR BREACH OF RULE 14-1 OR -2:
Match play – Loss of hole; Stroke play – Two strokes.

BALL TO BE FAIRLY STRUCK AT WITH CLUBHEAD

A player may strike the ball with the back or toe of the clubhead.

14-3. ARTIFICIAL DEVICES AND UNUSUAL EQUIPMENT

The United States Golf Association (USGA) reserves the right, at any time, to change the *Rules* relating to artificial devices and unusual equipment and make or change the interpretations relating to these Rules.

A player in doubt as to whether use of an item would constitute a breach of Rule 14-3 should consult the USGA.

A manufacturer may submit to the USGA a sample of an item to be manufactured for a ruling as to whether its use during a *stipulated round* would cause a player to be in breach of Rule 14-3. The sample becomes the property of the USGA for reference purposes. If a manufacturer fails to submit

CADDIE POSITIONED ON EXTENSION OF LINE OF PLAY BEHIND BALL

I will stay here to make sure you are correctly aligned while you are making your stroke.

If you remain there while I play my shot I will be penalized as I am not allowed to have my caddie positioned on an extension of the line of play behind my ball.

ASSISTANCE IN MAKING A STROKE

A player must not accept protection from the elements in making a stroke.

A player may protect himself from the elements in making a stroke.

a sample before manufacturing and/or marketing the item, the manufacturer assumes the risk of a ruling that use of the item would be contrary to the *Rules*.

Except as provided in the *Rules*, during a *stipulated round* the player must not use any artificial device or unusual equipment:

a. That might assist him in making a *stroke* or in his play; or

b. For the purpose of gauging or measuring distance or conditions that might affect his play; or

c. That might assist him in gripping the club, except that:

(i)   plain gloves may be worn;

(ii)   resin, powder and drying or moisturising agents may be used; and

(iii) a towel or handkerchief may be wrapped around the grip.

PENALTY FOR BREACH OF RULE 14-3:

Disqualification.

14-4. STRIKING THE BALL MORE THAN ONCE

See **incident** involving Rule 14-4 on page 61–2

If a player's club strikes the ball more than once in the course of a *stroke*, the player must count the *stroke* and **add a *penalty stroke***, making two *strokes* in all.

14-5. PLAYING MOVING BALL

A player must not make a *stroke* at his ball while it is moving.

Exceptions:

• Ball falling off *tee* – Rule 11-3

• Striking the ball more than once – Rule 14-4

• Ball moving in water – Rule 14-6

When the ball begins to *move* only after the player has begun the *stroke* or the backward movement of his club for the *stroke*, he incurs no penalty under this Rule for playing a moving ball, but he is not exempt from any penalty under the following *Rules*:

- Ball at rest *moved* by player – Rule 18-2a
- Ball at rest moving after *address* – Rule 18-2b

(Ball purposely deflected or stopped by player, *partner* or *caddie* – see Rule 1-2)

14-6. BALL MOVING IN WATER

When a ball is moving in water in a *water hazard*, the player may, without penalty, make a *stroke*, but he must not delay making his *stroke* in order to allow the wind or current to improve the position of the ball. A ball moving in water in a *water hazard* may be lifted if the player elects to invoke Rule 26.

PENALTY FOR BREACH OF RULE 14-5 OR 14-6:
Match play – Loss of hole; Stroke play – Two strokes.

RULE 14 INCIDENTS

Artificial devices, assistance from others, playing a ball before it is at rest, and striking it more than once are all conditions that alter a player relying solely on himself to fairly strike his golf ball. As such, they are prohibited under the Rules.

A player may hold an umbrella over his own head, but no one else may do this for him. A caddie may align a player at address, but must step away before the stroke is made. Binoculars can be used to identify a ball, but a range finder cannot be used to determine how far it is from the hole. Electronic devices taken onto the course may be used to obtain information about the Rules, the course, or any other matter published prior to the round. [Decision 14-3/16.]

At the 1999 U.S. Open at Pinehurst, Phil Mickelson made it clear that he would leave the field of competition, regardless of his position, if his wife went into labor with their first child. In order to be alerted to her situation, Mickelson carried a beeper with him during play. Although it was an artificial device, the beeper did not assist him in making a stroke or in his play and was, therefore, within the Rules.

No interpretation is necessary when a ball is struck more than once. From thick rough, short and right of Oakland Hills' 5th green during the 1985 U.S. Open, T.C. Chen encountered that unfortunate fluke in golf when one swing of the club strikes the ball more than once.

Chen's third shot had left his ball about 10 feet off the right front of the green and additional 10 feet to the hole. He was faced with a delicate pitch shot that needed enough clubhead speed to get the lofted club through the grass but not so much that the force imparted to the ball would cause it to run past the hole.

Practice swings left the necessary feeling in Chen's hands for gauging the grabbing effect of the grass. He addressed the ball and swung slowly but firmly. On the downswing, as the club approached the ball, the tall grass slowed the club. Chen firmly but gently pulled the club into the ball.

The ball came slowly off the decelerating clubface and rose ahead of it into the air. As the club finished its path through the grass, the resistance became less and the club was released. However, the firm pulling action still left in Chen's swing gave the club added momentum as it left the grass. In a spurt of speed, the club once again caught up with the slow-moving ball and collided with it a second time. As the ball ricocheted off the clubface, a spectator rose from his kneeling position directly behind Chen with two fingers raised, indicating that the ball had been struck twice.

As the lofted clubface was going up at the moment of second impact, the ball was pushed a little higher in the air and slightly to Chen's left. It came to rest on the apron of the putting green about 10 feet from the hole.

Rule 14-4 is clear in such a situation. "If a player's club strikes the ball more than once in the course of a stroke, the player shall count the stroke and add a penalty stroke, making two strokes in all."

Prior to the infraction, Chen led the championship by four strokes with 14 holes to play. Visibly shaken, he took three more to finish the hole for an eight. His hopes of winning the U.S. Open were dashed in the process. Indeed, he tied for second with Denis Watson and Dave Barr, just one shot behind Andy North.

One of golf's most infamous Rules situations involved T.C. Chen at the 1985 U.S. Open. This incident, which had a dramatic effect on the final results of the championship, is retold on this page.

PLAYING A SUBSTITUTED BALL

I lifted my ball from the putting green to clean it, but I have just noticed that I have played the other ball I had in my pocket.

Unfortunately, you have substituted a ball when not permitted to do so. It is now the ball in play and you incur a two-stroke penalty. If we had been playing a match you would have lost the hole.

RULE **15**

SUBSTITUTED BALL; WRONG BALL

DEFINITIONS

All defined terms are in *italics* and are listed alphabetically in the Definitions section – see pages 6–15.

15-1. GENERAL

A player must hole out with the ball played from the *teeing ground* unless the ball is *lost, out of bounds* or the player *substitutes* another ball, whether or not substitution is permitted (see Rule 15-2). If a player plays a *wrong ball*, see Rule 15-3.

15-2. SUBSTITUTED BALL

A player may *substitute* a ball when proceeding under a *Rule* that permits the player to play, drop or place another ball in completing the play of a hole. The *substituted ball* becomes the *ball in play*.

If a player substitutes a ball when not permitted to do so under the *Rules*, that *substituted ball* is not a *wrong ball*; it becomes the *ball in play*. If the mistake is not corrected as provided in Rule 20-6 and the player makes a *stroke* at a wrongly *substituted ball*, **he incurs the penalty prescribed by the applicable Rule** and, in stroke play, must play out the hole with the *substituted ball*. (Playing from Wrong Place – see Rule 20-7)

15-3. WRONG BALL
a. Match Play

If a player makes a *stroke* at a *wrong ball* that is not in a *hazard*, **he loses the hole**.

There is no penalty if a player makes a *stroke* at a *wrong ball* in a *hazard*. Any *strokes* made at a *wrong ball* in a *hazard* do not count in the player's score.

63

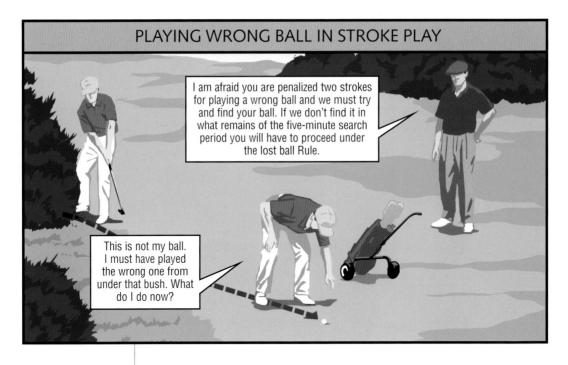

If the *wrong ball* belongs to another player, its owner must place a ball on the spot from which the *wrong ball* was first played.

If the player and opponent exchange balls during the play of a hole, the first to make a *stroke* at the *wrong ball* that is not in a *hazard* loses the hole; when this cannot be determined, the hole must be played out with the balls exchanged.

See **incident** involving Rule 15-3b below

b. Stroke Play

If a *competitor* makes a *stroke* or *strokes* at a *wrong ball* that is not in a *hazard*, **he incurs a penalty of two strokes**.

There is no penalty if a *competitor* makes a *stroke* at a *wrong ball* in a *hazard*. Any *strokes* made at a *wrong ball* in a *hazard* do not count in the *competitor's* score.

The *competitor* must correct his mistake by playing the correct ball or by proceeding under the *Rules*. If he fails to correct his mistake before making a *stroke* on the next *teeing ground* or, in the case of the last hole of the round, fails to declare his intention to correct his mistake before leaving the *putting green*, **he is disqualified**.

Strokes made by a *competitor* with a *wrong ball* do not count in his score.

If the *wrong ball* belongs to another *competitor*, its owner must place a ball on the spot from which the *wrong ball* was first played.

(Lie of ball to be placed or replaced altered – see Rule 20-3b)

(Spot not determinable – see Rule 20-3c)

RULE 15 INCIDENT

At the highest levels of competitive golf, it is rare that two players play each other's balls when both lie in the fairway. Brad Faxon and Phil Mickelson did exactly that at the 1995 Buick Invitational at Torrey Pines Golf Club in La Jolla, California.

Driving at the 1st hole (the player's 10th of the round, having started play on the back nine), both players' balls found the fairway. Their caddies walked ahead, lowered the respective bag at their player's ball, and made a club selection. Each then played to the putting green from an unremarkable fairway lie and walked ahead to putt.

Upon marking and lifting their balls on the green, Faxon and Mickelson were stunned to see they had each played the other's ball from the fairway. At this highest level of professional golf, for neither player nor neither caddie to notice the mix-up before playing to the green may have been partially due to the mundane nature of the situation. Had one or both of the balls been in the rough, a positive identification would more likely have been made before either or both second shots were struck. As it was, the balls were about 12 feet from each other in the fairway.

As stipulated by Rule 15, both Mickelson and Faxon had played a wrong ball. While the stroke each had made with the respective wrong ball did not count in their score, two penalty strokes were assessed to each player. Both men then placed a ball on the spot from which the wrong ball was first played (where their tee shots had come to rest) and completed the hole.

Because both players corrected their mistake before playing from the next tee, there was no danger of disqualification for this infraction. While the consequences for playing a wrong ball lie squarely with the player, it would be reasonable to assume after this infraction that a conversation about how such a mistake could have happened took place between the players and their caddies.

RULE 16

DEFINITIONS

See **incidents** involving Rule 16-1 on page 69

THE PUTTING GREEN

All defined terms are in *italics* and are listed alphabetically in the Definitions section – see pages 6–15.

16-1. GENERAL
a. Touching Line of Putt
The line of putt must not be touched except:
(i) the player may remove *loose impediments*, provided he does not press anything down;
(ii) the player may place the club in front of the ball when *addressing* it, provided he does not press anything down;
(iii) in measuring – Rule 18-6;
(iv) in lifting the ball – Rule 16-1b;
(v) in pressing down a ball-marker;
(vi) in repairing old *hole* plugs or ball marks on the *putting green* – Rule 16-1c; and
(vii) in removing movable *obstructions* – Rule 24-1
(Indicating line for putting on *putting green* – see Rule 8-2b)

b. Lifting and Cleaning Ball
A ball on the *putting green* may be lifted and, if desired, cleaned. The

65

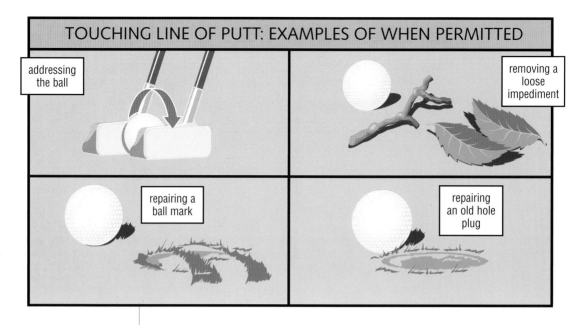

position of the ball must be marked before it is lifted and the ball must be replaced (see Rule 20-1).

c. Repair of Hole Plugs, Ball Marks and Other Damage

The player may repair an old *hole* plug or damage to the *putting green* caused by the impact of a ball, whether or not the player's ball lies on the *putting green*. If a ball or ball-marker is accidentally *moved* in the process of the repair, the ball or ball-marker must be replaced. There is no penalty provided the

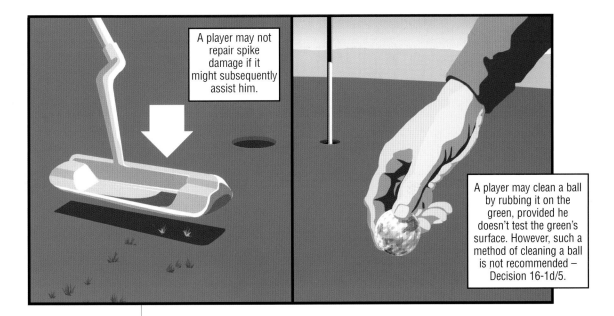

A player may not repair spike damage if it might subsequently assist him.

A player may clean a ball by rubbing it on the green, provided he doesn't test the green's surface. However, such a method of cleaning a ball is not recommended – Decision 16-1d/5.

movement of the ball is directly attributable to the specific act of repairing an old *hole* plug or damage to the *putting green* caused by the impact of a ball. Otherwise, **the player incurs a *penalty stroke* under Rule 18-2a.**

Any other damage to the *putting green* must not be repaired if it might assist the player in his subsequent play of the hole.

d. Testing Surface

During the play of a hole, a player must not test the surface of the *putting green* by rolling a ball or roughening or scraping the surface.

REMOVING LOOSE IMPEDIMENTS FROM LINE OF PUTT

Can I remove these leaves using my cap rather than my hand?

Yes, loose impediments can be removed from your line of putt by any means provided you do not press anything down.

e. Standing Astride or on Line of Putt

The player must not make a *stroke* on the *putting green* from a stance astride, or with either foot touching, the *line of putt* or an extension of that line behind the ball.

f. Making Stroke While Another Ball in Motion

The player must not make a *stroke* while another ball is in motion after a *stroke* from the *putting green*, except that, if a player does so, there is no penalty if it was his turn to play.

(Lifting ball assisting or interfering with play while another ball in motion – see Rule 22)

PENALTY FOR BREACH OF RULE 16-1:

Match play – Loss of hole; Stroke play – Two strokes.

(Position of *caddie* or *partner* – see Rule 14-2)

(Wrong *putting green* – see Rule 25-3)

16-2. BALL OVERHANGING HOLE

See **incidents** involving Rule 16-2 on page 69–70

When any part of the ball overhangs the lip of the *hole*, the player is allowed enough time to reach the *hole* without unreasonable delay and an additional ten seconds to determine whether the ball is at rest. If by then the ball has

BALL OVERHANGING HOLE

How long may I wait to see if my ball will fall into the hole?

There's no point in waiting more than ten seconds. After that time the ball is deemed to be at rest and if it then falls in you have holed out with your last stroke, but you add a penalty stroke.

not fallen into the *hole*, it is deemed to be at rest. If the ball subsequently falls into the *hole*, the player is deemed to have *holed* out with his last *stroke*, and **he must add a *penalty stroke* to his score** for the hole; otherwise, there is no penalty under this Rule.

(Undue delay – see Rule 6-7)

RULE 16 INCIDENTS

The line of putt is protected under the Rules so that it is left as unaltered as possible before a putt is played. The seven times that the line can be touched are laid out in Rule 16-1. As a change to the Rules in 2004, removing loose impediments on the line of putt can now be done by any method, providing that the line is not improved as a result. Prior to this change, they could only be removed by picking them up or brushing them aside using a club or your hand.

When Vijah Singh used a towel to remove sand from the putting green at the 2003 Wachovia Championship, it ultimately cost him the chance of forcing a playoff.

Singh was playing the par-5 15th hole during the first round of the tournament at Quail Hollow in Charlotte, North Carolina. His second shot reached the green, and he walked ahead as his fellow-competitors, Nick Price and Brad Faxon, played their third shots to the green. Singh waited about 20 yards in front of Price and Faxon and, after they played their third shots, Singh walked onto the green.

As is his custom, the Fijian often carries a towel over his shoulder that he uses to mop perspiration. Sand from a greenside bunker was on the line of Singh's 40-foot eagle putt. He instinctively pulled the towel from his shoulder and used it to swat the sand away and clear his line to the hole.

Walking to the green, Price and Faxon saw what looked like an infraction. When they reached Singh, Faxon asked if Singh had touched or moved anything on his line. Singh said he had, and Faxon told him he couldn't do that. Steve Rintoul, a PGA Tour rules official, was called to confer on the ruling. Singh confirmed that he had touched his line with the towel and that the sand had been moved with the towel.

After the ensuing two-stroke penalty was applied, Singh was left putting for par rather than eagle. He two putted and made bogey. Ironically, on the final day of the tournament, David Toms came to the 72nd hole with a six-stroke lead, and made a quadruple bogey to win by two strokes over Singh.

The Rule dealing with a ball overhanging the hole [Rule 16-2] was revised as a result of an incident involving Denis Watson at Oakland Hills' 8th hole during the 1985 U.S. Open.

From 10 feet, Watson putted and his ball stopped on the lip of the hole. After waiting an extended period of time, the ball fell in. Subsequently, Watson was told to add two penalty strokes to his score for undue delay, as described at the time in Rule 16-1h.

The severe ramification of the penalty would not be clear for three more days when Watson would finish just one stroke behind the champion, Andy North.

In 1988, the Rule was moved to Rule 16-2 and a one-stroke penalty assigned to its infraction. However, Brian Gay discovered at the 2000 Honda Classic that the application of Rule 16 is literal and the ramifications can still be severe.

On the 17th hole of the final round, Gay found himself needing a 30-foot birdie putt to draw even with Dudley Hart, who had just finished his round with a tap-in birdie at the 18th. Gay played a smooth, well-read putt, which finished on the edge of the front lip of the hole.

Gay walked to the hole, waited 13 seconds and then watched as the ball fell in. The scoreboard recorded a birdie and Gay played the final hole believing a two-putt par would force a playoff. From 100 feet away, Gay three putted the 18th and the victory was Hart's.

As it turned out, however, Gay had not birdied the 17th because he had incurred a penalty stroke under Rule 16-2. After multiple viewings of the videotape, it was clear to the PGA Tour Rules Official, Slugger White, that there was an infraction, and Gay had to sign for a par 4 at the 17th rather than a three.

"I looked at the tape 10 times," White said, "and [Gay] and I looked at the tape another five or six times. We rolled it, we backed it up, we did everything."

The infraction was clear to the official. "It's not something you like to do," said White. "But in all honesty, he walked up to the hole. He didn't run to the hole. He did exactly what he was supposed to do."

While the three putt at the 18th had eliminated Gay's chance of winning, the penalty stroke moved him from a tie for second to a tie for fourth.

RULE **17**

THE FLAGSTICK

DEFINITIONS

All defined terms are in *italics* and are listed alphabetically in the Definitions section – see pages 6–15.

17-1. FLAGSTICK ATTENDED, REMOVED OR HELD UP

Before making a *stroke* from anywhere on the *course*, the player may have the *flagstick* attended, removed or held up to indicate the position of the *hole*.

If the *flagstick* is not attended, removed or held up before the player makes a *stroke*, it must not be attended, removed or held up during the *stroke* or while the player's ball is in motion if doing so might influence the movement of the ball.

Note 1: If the *flagstick* is in the *hole* and anyone stands near it while a *stroke* is being made, he is deemed to be attending the *flagstick*.

Note 2: If, prior to the *stroke*, the *flagstick* is attended, removed or held up by anyone with the player's knowledge and he makes no objection, the player is deemed to have authorized it.

Note 3: If anyone attends or holds up the *flagstick* while a *stroke* is being made, he is deemed to be attending the *flagstick* until the ball comes to rest.

17-2. UNAUTHORIZED ATTENDANCE

If an opponent or his *caddie* in match play or a *fellow-competitor* or his *caddie* in stroke play, without the player's authority or prior knowledge, attends, removes or holds up the *flagstick* during the *stroke* or while the ball is in motion, and the act might influence the movement of the ball, the opponent or *fellow-competitor* incurs the applicable penalty.

PENALTY FOR BREACH OF RULE 17-1 OR 17-2
Match play – Loss of hole; Stroke play – Two strokes.

*In stroke play, if a breach of Rule 17-2 occurs and the *competitor's* ball subsequently strikes the *flagstick*, the person attending or holding it or anything carried by him, the *competitor* incurs no penalty. The ball is played as it lies except that, if the *stroke* was made on the *putting green*, the *stroke* is cancelled and the ball must be replaced and replayed.

17-3. BALL STRIKING FLAGSTICK OR ATTENDANT

The player's ball must not strike:
a. The *flagstick* when it is being attended, removed or held up;
b. The person attending or holding up the *flagstick*; or
c. The *flagstick* in the *hole*, unattended, when the *stroke* has been made on the *putting green*.

Exception: When the *flagstick* is attended, removed or held up without the player's authority – see Rule 17-2.

PENALTY FOR BREACH OF RULE 17-3:
Match play – Loss of hole; Stroke play – Two strokes and the ball must be played as it lies.

See **incidents** involving Rule 17-3 on page 73

71

17-4. BALL RESTING AGAINST FLAGSTICK

When the *flagstick* is in the *hole* and a player's ball when not *holed* rests against it, the player or another person authorized by him may move or remove the *flagstick* and if the ball falls into the *hole*, the player is deemed to have *holed* out with his last *stroke*; otherwise, the ball, if *moved*, must be placed on the lip of the *hole*, without penalty.

RULE 17 INCIDENTS

Rule 4 stipulates the characteristics of a golf club, but nowhere in the Rules is it stated where a particular club must be used. Any club can be used anywhere. Habit, however, sometimes lulls into penalty situations that would otherwise appear obvious.

A putter is designed for putting, and is primarily used on the putting green. When a player, with putter in hand, approaches their ball on the green, certain Rules come to mind that are unique to the putting green, such as the right to lift and clean a ball in play, the repair of ball marks and old hole plugs, and the prohibition against making a putt with the flagstick in the hole.

When a player decides to use a club other than a putter on the green their rights and obligations under the Rules are sometimes less instinctive.

During the final match of the 2002 U.S. Mid-Amateur Championship at The Stanwich Club in Greenwich, Connecticut, George Zahringer found himself so distracted. Zahringer's shot from the tee to the 199-yard 13th hole finished on the front left corner of the green. The hole was cut in a back left position, and a bunker lay directly between Zahringer's ball and the hole.

Stanwich is Zahringer's home club and he was aware that, while it was possible to putt, such a play would at best finish about 15 feet from hole. For this reason, he decided to pitch the ball. Having selected a wedge for the stroke, Zahringer, his caddie and others attending the match focused on the pitch to be played and overlooked the need to attend or remove the flagstick. [Rule 17-3.]

The shape and contours of the 17th green at Pebble Beach Golf Links resulted in an unusual sight at the 2000 U.S. Open. For the details of this incident, involving eventual runner-up Miguel Angel Jimenez, see the story on the next page.

Zahringer pitched well, to within two feet of the hole, but not too well, holing the shot or striking the flagstick. His three was good enough to win the hole from Jerry Courville, his opponent, who three-putted from the center of the green for bogey.

Had Zahringer's pitch from the green struck the flagstick, the penalty would have been loss of hole, and the match would have moved to the 14th hole with Zahringer, the eventual champion, 1 up rather than 3 up.

As Zahringer's situation illustrates, golf requires imagination and some holes and conditions demand more than others. At Pebble Beach's par-3 17th hole, during the 2000 U.S. Open, Miguel Angel Jimenez found himself in a situation similar to Zahringer's. When H. Chandler Egan made design changes to the course prior to the 1929 U.S. Amateur Championship, one of those changes included redesigning the 17th green into the shape of an hourglass divided by a diagonal ridge. The ridge running across the center of the green has the effect of creating a double green. Hence, when the hole is cut at point B [see illustration], it is difficult for a ball played from point A to get close to the hole. This was Jimenez's dilemma.

The pinched, hourglass shape brought the rough into the line of putt necessary for him to get close to the hole. Like Zahringer, Jimenez chose to play a pitch shot from the green, over the rough and the ridge, to the hole on the other side.

Jimenez was aware of the Rules regarding the flagstick, and wisely sought confirmation from the Rules official walking with his group. In order to avoid an infraction caused by his ball striking the flagstick, he directed his caddie to attend the flagstick.

Rule 17-3a also states that it is an infraction for a ball to strike an attended flagstick regardless of from where the shot has been played. The penalty in stroke play is two strokes. Therefore, Jimenez's caddie was directed to remove the flagstick if it looked as though the ball might strike it or go into the hole.

Playing a delicate pitch, Jimenez took a small divot. His ball landed on the down slope of the ridge and ran to about 10 feet from the hole. From there he took two putts for bogey.

RULE 18 — BALL AT REST MOVED

DEFINITIONS All defined terms are in *italics* and are listed alphabetically in the Definitions section – see pages 6–15.

18-1. BY OUTSIDE AGENCY
If a ball at rest is *moved* by an *outside agency*, there is no penalty and the ball must be replaced.
(Player's ball at rest *moved* by another ball – see Rule 18-5)

See **incidents** involving Rule 18-2a on page 78

18-2. BY PLAYER, PARTNER, CADDIE OR EQUIPMENT
a. General
When a player's ball is *in play*, if:

BALL AT REST MOVED

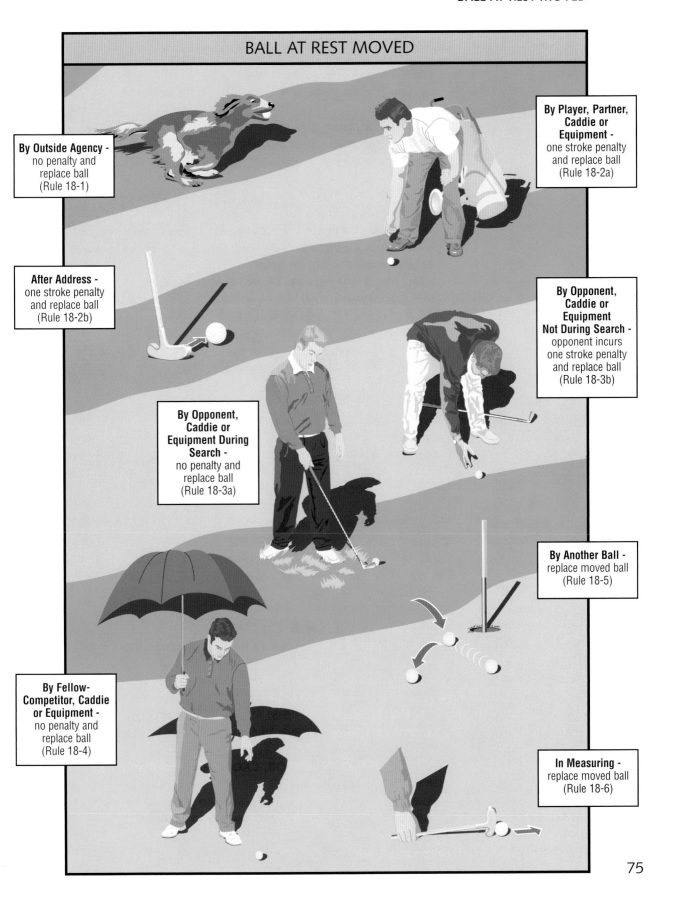

By Outside Agency - no penalty and replace ball (Rule 18-1)

By Player, Partner, Caddie or Equipment - one stroke penalty and replace ball (Rule 18-2a)

After Address - one stroke penalty and replace ball (Rule 18-2b)

By Opponent, Caddie or Equipment Not During Search - opponent incurs one stroke penalty and replace ball (Rule 18-3b)

By Opponent, Caddie or Equipment During Search - no penalty and replace ball (Rule 18-3a)

By Another Ball - replace moved ball (Rule 18-5)

By Fellow-Competitor, Caddie or Equipment - no penalty and replace ball (Rule 18-4)

In Measuring - replace moved ball (Rule 18-6)

(i)   the player, his *partner* or either of their *caddies* lifts or *moves* it, touches it purposely (except with a club in the act of *addressing* it) or causes it to *move* except as permitted by a *Rule*, or

(ii) *equipment* of the player or his *partner* causes the ball to *move*,

the player incurs a penalty of one stroke. If the ball is *moved*, it must be replaced unless the movement of the ball occurs after the player has begun the *stroke* or the backward movement of the club for the *stroke* and the *stroke* is made.

Under the *Rules* there is no penalty if a player accidentally causes his ball to *move* in the following circumstances:

In searching for a ball in a *hazard* covered by *loose impediments* or sand, for a ball in an *abnormal ground condition* or for a ball believed to be in a *water hazard* – Rule 12-1

In repairing a *hole* plug or ball mark – Rule 16-1c

In measuring – Rule 18-6

In lifting a ball under a *Rule* – Rule 20-1

In placing or replacing a ball under a *Rule* – Rule 20-3a

In removing a *loose impediment* on the *putting green* – Rule 23-1

In removing movable *obstructions* – Rule 24-1

See **incidents** involving Rule 18-2b on page 78

b. Ball Moving After Address

If a player's *ball in play moves* after he has *addressed* it (other than as a result of a *stroke*), the player is deemed to have *moved* the ball and **incurs a penalty of one stroke**. The ball must be replaced unless the movement of the ball occurs after the player has begun the *stroke* or the backward movement of the club for the *stroke* and the *stroke* is made.

18-3. BY OPPONENT, CADDIE OR EQUIPMENT IN MATCH PLAY
a. During Search

If, during search for a player's ball, an opponent, his *caddie* or his *equipment moves* the ball, touches it or causes it to *move*, there is no penalty. If the ball is *moved*, it must be replaced.

b. Other Than During Search

If, other than during search for a player's ball, an opponent, his *caddie* or his *equipment moves* the ball, touches it purposely or causes it to *move*, except as otherwise provided in the *Rules*, **the opponent incurs a penalty of one stroke**. If the ball is *moved*, it must be replaced.

(Playing a *wrong ball* - see Rule 15-3)

(Ball moved in measuring - see Rule 18-6)

18-4. BY FELLOW-COMPETITOR, CADDIE OR EQUIPMENT IN STROKE PLAY

If a *fellow-competitor*, his *caddie* or his *equipment moves* the player's ball, touches it or causes it to *move*, there is no penalty. If the ball is *moved*, it must be replaced.

(Playing a *wrong ball* - see Rule 15-3).

See **incidents** involving Rule 18-5 below

18-5. BY ANOTHER BALL

If a *ball in play* and at rest is *moved* by another ball in motion after a *stroke*, the *moved* ball must be replaced.

18-6. BALL MOVED IN MEASURING

If a ball or ball-marker is *moved* in measuring while proceeding under or in determining the application of a *Rule*, the ball or ball-marker must be replaced. There is no penalty provided the movement of the ball or ball-marker is directly attributable to the specific act of measuring. Otherwise, **the provisions of Rules 18-2a, 18-3b, or 18-4 apply.**

PENALTY FOR BREACH OF RULE:
Match play - Loss of hole; Stroke play - Two strokes.
*If a player who is required to replace a ball fails to do so, he incurs the general penalty for breach of Rule 18. There is no additional penalty under Rule 18, except in the case of a wrongly *substituted ball* (Rule 15-2).

Note 1: If a ball to be replaced under this Rule is not immediately recoverable, another ball may be *substituted*.
Note 2: If the original lie of a ball to be placed or replaced has been altered, see Rule 20-3b.
Note 3: If it is impossible to determine the spot on which a ball is to be placed, see Rule 20-3c.

RULE 18 INCIDENTS

Rules 18 and 22 collided during the first round of the U.S. Senior Open just as Hubert Green and Bob Murphy's golf balls did in a fairway bunker at the 17th hole.

Murphy drove into the bunker, and Green's drive followed Murphy's exactly. Murphy's ball at rest was struck and moved by Green's ball. A volunteer marshal witnessed the collision and informed the walking Rules Official. Tracks made by the balls in the sand confirmed the marshal's report, as well as the location from which Murphy's ball had been moved.

Neither player was penalized, but Murphy was required to replace his ball at the spot from which it was moved. [Rule 18-5.] Green's ball had to be played as it lay. [Rule 19-5.] From the tracks in the sand, it was clear that when Murphy replaced his ball it would interfere with Green's play. Entitled to the removal of Murphy's ball [Rule 22], Green requested to play before Murphy's ball was replaced. Murphy marked the original location of his ball with a tee, and Green played.

A player is not permitted to clean his ball when it is lifted under Rule 22. However, in this case, Rule 18 took precedence over Rule 22. Anywhere on the golf course, a ball moved by another ball may be cleaned before being replaced to its original location. After Green's play, Murphy was required to recreate his original lie in the bunker, place his ball in that lie, and then play out.

During the first round of the 1925 U.S. Open at Worcester C.C. in Massachusetts, Bobby Jones saw his ball move after he addressed it on a steep bank at the 11th hole. Jones added a penalty stroke to his score.

When praised for his honesty, Jones replied, "You just might as well praise me for not breaking into banks. There is only one way to play this game." Jones began the final round in a tie for fourth place and was able to tie Willie Macfarlane to force a 36-hole playoff, which Jones lost 75-73 to Macfarlane's 75-72.

While leading the first round of the 1992 U.S. Women's Open at Oakmont C.C. in Pittsburgh, Donna Andrews' ball was on the apron just over the 17th putting green. Tall rough crowded the ball at the back. As she practiced the stroke for her difficult putt, her club unintentionally bumped and moved her ball about five inches. Realizing her error, Andrews gathered her concentration and finished the hole from the ball's new location.

Because she had not intended to strike her ball, a stroke, as defined by the Rules, had had not been made. Two penalty strokes were levied against Andrews for causing her ball to move and not replacing it before playing again. [Rule 18-2a.] Her infraction had been televised and Andrews was alerted to her penalty before signing and returning her card without including the penalty, which would have resulted in her disqualification. [Rule 6-6d.]

Davis Love III was not so fortunate during The 1997 Players Championship. While going through his pre-shot routine prior to putting on the 17th green, Love's putter accidentally moved his ball about an inch. Failing to replace the moved ball, he, like Andrews, continued putting from the new spot and then moved to the 18th tee. Assessing himself one stroke for moving the ball rather than the total penalty of two strokes for moving and not replacing his ball, Love recorded a four on his card instead of a five.

Although viewed by thousands of spectators, the error was not brought to Love's attention until after he returned his scorecard. The result was disqualification.

RULE 19 — BALL IN MOTION DEFLECTED OR STOPPED

DEFINITIONS

All defined terms are in *italics* and are listed alphabetically in the Definitions section – see pages 6–15.

19-1. BY OUTSIDE AGENCY

See **incident** involving Rule 19-1 on page 81

If a ball in motion is accidentally deflected or stopped by any *outside agency*, it is a *rub of the green*, there is no penalty and the ball must be played as it lies except:

a. If a ball in motion after a *stroke* other than on the *putting green* comes to rest in or on any moving or animate *outside agency*, the player must, *through the green* or in a *hazard*, drop the ball, or on the *putting green* place the ball, as near as possible to the spot where the *outside agency* was when the ball came to rest in or on it, and

b. If a ball in motion after a *stroke* on the *putting green* is deflected or stopped by, or comes to rest in or on, any moving or animate *outside agency* except a worm or an insect, the *stroke* is cancelled. The ball must be replaced

BALL IN MOTION DEFLECTED OR STOPPED

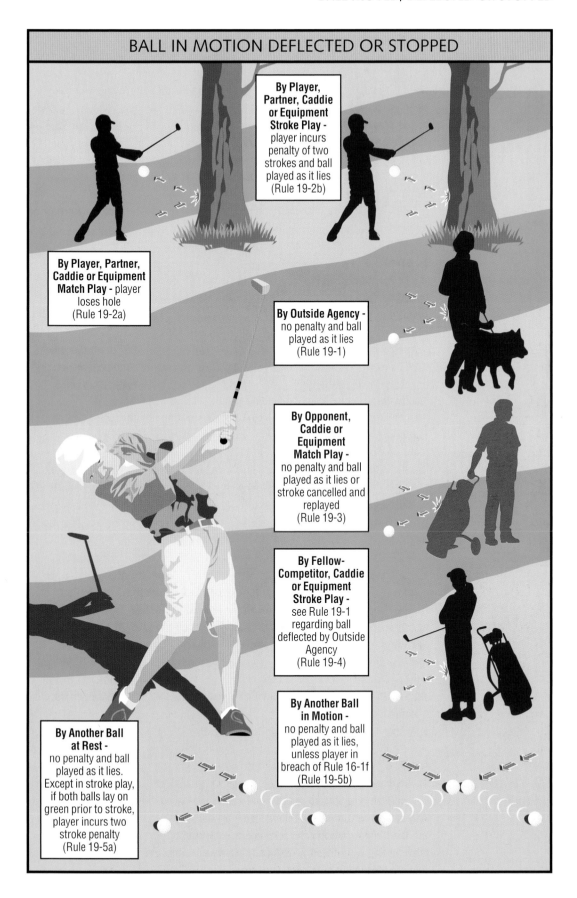

By Player, Partner, Caddie or Equipment Stroke Play - player incurs penalty of two strokes and ball played as it lies (Rule 19-2b)

By Player, Partner, Caddie or Equipment Match Play - player loses hole (Rule 19-2a)

By Outside Agency - no penalty and ball played as it lies (Rule 19-1)

By Opponent, Caddie or Equipment Match Play - no penalty and ball played as it lies or stroke cancelled and replayed (Rule 19-3)

By Fellow-Competitor, Caddie or Equipment Stroke Play - see Rule 19-1 regarding ball deflected by Outside Agency (Rule 19-4)

By Another Ball in Motion - no penalty and ball played as it lies, unless player in breach of Rule 16-1f (Rule 19-5b)

By Another Ball at Rest - no penalty and ball played as it lies. Except in stroke play, if both balls lay on green prior to stroke, player incurs two stroke penalty (Rule 19-5a)

79

and the *stroke* replayed.

If the ball is not immediately recoverable, another ball may be *substituted*.
(Player's ball deflected or stopped by another ball – see Rule 19-5)

Note: If the *referee* or the *Committee* determines that a player's ball has been purposely deflected or stopped by an *outside agency*, Rule 1-4 applies to the player. If the *outside agency* is a *fellow-competitor* or his *caddie*, Rule 1-2 applies to the *fellow-competitor*.

19-2. BY PLAYER, PARTNER, CADDIE OR EQUIPMENT
a. Match Play

If a player's ball is accidentally deflected or stopped by himself, his *partner* or either of their *caddies* or *equipment*, **he loses the hole**.

b. Stroke Play

See **incident** involving Rule 19-2 on page 81

If a *competitor's* ball is accidentally deflected or stopped by himself, his *partner* or either of their *caddies* or *equipment*, **the *competitor* incurs a penalty of two strokes**. The ball must be played as it lies, except when it comes to rest in or on the *competitor's*, his *partner's* or either of their *caddies'* clothes or *equipment*, in which case the *competitor* must *through the green* or in a *hazard* drop the ball, or on the *putting green* place the ball, as near as possible to where the article was when the ball came to rest in or on it.

Exception: Dropped ball – see Rule 20-2a.

(Ball purposely deflected or stopped by player, *partner* or *caddie* – see Rule 1-2)

19-3. BY OPPONENT, CADDIE OR EQUIPMENT IN MATCH PLAY

If a player's ball is accidentally deflected or stopped by an opponent, his *caddie* or his *equipment*, there is no penalty. The player may, before another *stroke* is played by either *side*, cancel the *stroke* and play a ball without penalty as nearly as possible at the spot from which the original ball was last played (see Rule 20-5) or he may play the ball as it lies. However, if the player elects not to cancel the *stroke* and the ball has come to rest in or on the opponent's or his *caddie's* clothes or *equipment*, the player must *through the green* or in a *hazard* drop the ball, or on the *putting green* place the ball, as near as possible to where the article was when the ball came to rest in or on it.

Exception: Ball striking person attending *flagstick* – see Rule 17-3b.

(Ball purposely deflected or stopped by opponent or *caddie* – see Rule 1-2)

19-4. BY FELLOW-COMPETITOR, CADDIE OR EQUIPMENT IN STROKE PLAY

See Rule 19-1 regarding ball deflected by *outside agency*.

19-5. BY ANOTHER BALL
a. At Rest

If a player's ball in motion after a *stroke* is deflected or stopped by a *ball in play* and at rest, the player must play his ball as it lies. In match play, there is no penalty. In stroke play, there is no penalty unless both balls lay on the *putting green* prior to the *stroke*, in which case **the player incurs a penalty of two strokes**.

b. In Motion

If a player's ball in motion after a *stroke* is deflected or stopped by another ball in motion after a *stroke*, the player must play his ball as it lies. There is no penalty unless the player was in breach of Rule 16-1f, in which case **he incurs the penalty for breach of that Rule**.

Exception: If the player's ball is in motion after a *stroke* on the *putting green* and the other ball in motion is an *outside agency* – see Rule 19-1b.

PENALTY FOR BREACH OF RULE:

Match play – Loss of hole; Stroke play – Two strokes.

RULE 19 INCIDENTS

"I guess my reflexes aren't what they used to be," Jeff Maggert said reflecting on his ball hitting him in the chest during the final round of the 2003 Masters.

By Sunday, the shortest two-shot hole at Augusta National had sufficiently dried from its previously soggy condition so that Maggert chose a 2-iron from the tee in order to avoid the fairway bunkers or an awkward lie further along in the fairway. Regardless of his caution, his ball found one of the four fairway bunkers on the left.

The Committee prepares the bunkers at Augusta with a distinctively high lip, which can prove difficult to negotiate in certain situations. Maggert, however, was far enough from the lip and close enough to the green that his choice of a 52-degree wedge removed his concern about the lip.

Striking the ball a bit thin reduced its launch angle from the sand. The ball struck the lip and ricocheted directly back at Maggert striking him in the chest. It was not clear from the television camera angle behind Maggert if the ball had actually struck him. Maggert immediately acknowledged the violation, and was assessed a two-stroke penalty. [Rule 19-2.] He would finish in fifth place, five shots behind Mike Weir.

Rub of the green is a term within the Rules that only appears when any outside agency accidentally deflects or stops a ball in motion. [Rule 19-1.] Tom Kite found his chances to capture the 2001 Fleet Boston Classic foiled when his ball struck a bird during the final round of the senior event.

After four consecutive birdies, Kite came to Nashawtuc C.C.'s 167-yard par-3 17th with a share of the lead. Kite's iron shot from the tee was so purely struck that he didn't watch it. "It was blanketing the flag," Champions Tour Official Joe Terry recalls, "and then it disappeared. Tom asked me where the ball had ended up, and I told him I didn't know. It was missing. We were both puzzled. Only the greenside marshal, who's job it was to mark where errant balls last crossed the margin of the hazard, had seen the ball strike a bird in the air and then fall into the lateral water hazard next to the green."

After speaking to the marshal, Terry radioed the television production trailer and was able to determine that the collision had been recorded and could be reviewed. Somewhat disoriented by the quick turn of events, Kite had the presence of mind to ask Terry not to leave him. "Tom said,

'Don't leave me. I'm in brain shock, and I don't want to proceed incorrectly,'" Terry remembers. "and that was impressive."

When Kite's ball struck the bird and was deflected into the hazard, it was a rub of the green. With his ball lying in the lateral water hazard, and not wanting to play it, Kite had to proceed under Rule 26. His best option was to drop behind the hazard, keeping the point at which the ball last crossed the margin between the hole and dropping point. [Rule 26-1b.] He got up and down from 35 yards for a bogey four, and finished four shots behind eventual winner Larry Nelson.

Part of golf's enigma is that it is filled with unpredictable bounces and results, sometimes fortuitous, sometimes not. The outcome for Kite in Boston might seem inequitable, however, had the bird deflected the ball into the hole, it would have been a hole-in-one.

RULE **20**

LIFTING, DROPPING AND PLACING; PLAYING FROM WRONG PLACE

DEFINITIONS All defined terms are in *italics* and are listed alphabetically in the Definitions section – see pages 6–15.

20-1. LIFTING AND MARKING

See **incidents** involving Rule 20-1 on page 89–90

A ball to be lifted under the *Rules* may be lifted by the player, his *partner* or another person authorized by the player. In any such case, the player is responsible for any breach of the *Rules*.

The position of the ball must be marked before it is lifted under a *Rule* that requires it to be replaced. If it is not marked, **the player incurs a penalty of one stroke** and the ball must be replaced. If it is not replaced, **the player incurs the general penalty for breach of this Rule** but there is no additional penalty under Rule 20-1.

If a ball or ball-marker is accidentally *moved* in the process of lifting the ball under a *Rule* or marking its position, the ball or ball-marker must be replaced. There is no penalty provided the movement of the ball or ball-marker is directly attributable to the specific act of marking the position of or lifting the ball. Otherwise, **the player incurs a penalty of one stroke** under this Rule or Rule 18-2a.

Exception: If a player incurs a penalty for failing to act in accordance with Rule 5-3 or 12-2, there is no additional penalty under Rule 20-1.

Note: The position of a ball to be lifted should be marked by placing a ball-marker, a small coin or other similar object immediately behind the ball. If the ball-marker interferes with the play, *stance* or *stroke* of another player, it should be placed one or more clubhead-lengths to one side.

20-2. DROPPING AND RE-DROPPING
a. By Whom and How

See **incident** involving Rule 20-2a on page 89

A ball to be dropped under the *Rules* must be dropped by the player himself. He must stand erect, hold the ball at shoulder height and arm's length and drop it. If a ball is dropped by any other person or in any other manner and

PROCEDURE FOR LIFTING BALL

HOW TO DROP BALL

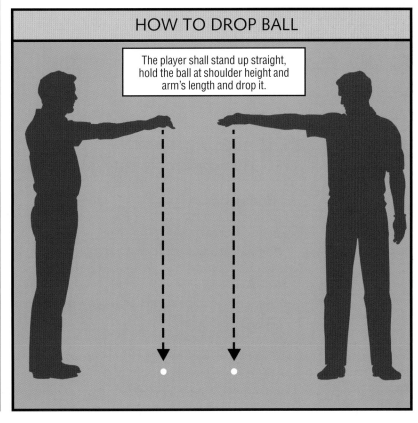

83

the error is not corrected as provided in Rule 20-6, **the player incurs a penalty of one stroke**.

If the ball touches the player, his *partner*, either of their *caddies* or their *equipment* before or after it strikes a part of the *course*, the ball must be re-dropped, without penalty. There is no limit to the number of times a ball must be re-dropped in these circumstances.

(Taking action to influence position or movement of ball – see Rule 1-2)

b. Where to Drop

When a ball is to be dropped as near as possible to a specific spot, it must be dropped not nearer the *hole* than the specific spot which, if it is not precisely known to the player, must be estimated.

A ball when dropped must first strike a part of the *course* where the applicable *Rule* requires it to be dropped. If it is not so dropped, Rules 20-6 and -7 apply.

c. When to Re-Drop

A dropped ball must be re-dropped without penalty if it:
(i)   rolls into and comes to rest in a *hazard*;
(ii)   rolls out of and comes to rest outside a *hazard*;
(iii)   rolls onto and comes to rest on a *putting green*;
(iv)   rolls and comes to rest *out of bounds*;
(v)   rolls to and comes to rest in a position where there is interference by the condition from which relief was taken under Rule 24-2b (*immovable obstruction*), Rule 25-1 (*abnormal ground conditions*), Rule 25-3 (*wrong putting green*) or a Local Rule (Rule 33-8a), or rolls back into the pitch-mark from which it was lifted under Rule 25-2 (*embedded ball*);
(vi)   rolls and comes to rest more than two club-lengths from where it first struck a part of the *course*; or
(vii)   rolls and comes to rest nearer the *hole* than:
(a) its original position or estimated position (see Rule 20-2b) unless otherwise permitted by the *Rules*; or
(b) the *nearest point of relief* or maximum available relief (Rule 24-2, 25-1 or 25-3); or
(c) the point where the original ball last crossed the margin of the *water hazard* or *lateral water hazard* (Rule 26-1).

If the ball when re-dropped rolls into any position listed above, it must be placed as near as possible to the spot where it first struck a part of the *course* when re-dropped.

If a ball to be re-dropped or placed under this Rule is not immediately recoverable, another ball may be *substituted*.

Note: If a ball when dropped or re-dropped comes to rest and subsequently *moves*, the ball must be played as it lies, unless the provisions of any other *Rule* apply.

20-3. PLACING AND REPLACING
a. By Whom and Where

A ball to be placed under the *Rules* must be placed by the player or his *partner*. If a ball is to be replaced, the player, his *partner* or the person who

See **incident** involving Rule 20-3 on page 89–90

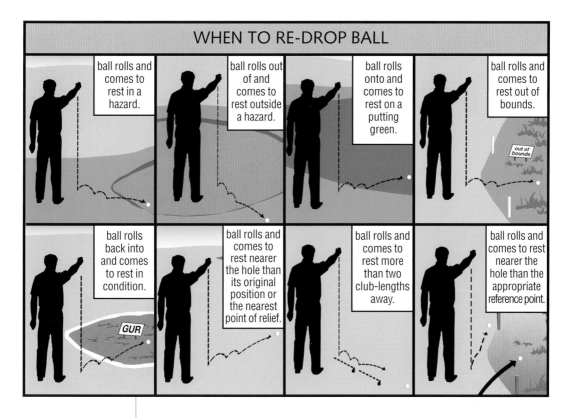

lifted or *moved* it must place it on the spot from which it was lifted or *moved*. In any such case, the player is responsible for any breach of the *Rules*.

If a ball or ball-marker is accidentally *moved* in the process of placing or replacing the ball, the ball or ball-marker must be replaced. There is no penalty provided the movement of the ball or ball-marker is directly attributable to the specific act of placing or replacing the ball or removing the ball-marker. Otherwise, **the player incurs a *penalty stroke*** under Rule 18-2a or 20-1.

b. Lie of Ball to be Placed or Replaced Altered

If the original lie of a ball to be placed or replaced has been altered:

(i)   except in a *hazard*, the ball must be placed in the nearest lie most similar to the original lie that is not more than one club-length from the original lie, not nearer the *hole* and not in a *hazard*;

(ii) in a *water hazard*, the ball must be placed in accordance with Clause (i) above, except that the ball must be placed in the *water hazard*;

(iii) in a *bunker*, the original lie must be re-created as nearly as possible and the ball must be placed in that lie.

c. Spot Not Determinable

If it is impossible to determine the spot where the ball is to be placed or replaced:

(i)   *through the green*, the ball must be dropped as near as possible to the place where it lay but not in a *hazard* or on a *putting green*;

(ii) in a *hazard*, the ball must be dropped in the *hazard* as near as possible to the place where it lay;

(iii)   on the *putting green*, the ball must be placed as near as possible to the place where it lay but not in a *hazard*.

Exception: When resuming play (Rule 6-8d), if the spot where the ball is to be placed is impossible to determine, it must be estimated and the ball placed on the estimated spot.

d. Ball Fails to Come to Rest on Spot

If a ball when placed fails to come to rest on the spot on which it was placed, there is no penalty and the ball must be replaced. If it still fails to come to rest on that spot:

(i)   except in a *hazard*, it must be placed at the nearest spot where it can be placed at rest that is not nearer the *hole* and not in a *hazard*;

(ii)   in a *hazard*, it must be placed in the *hazard* at the nearest spot where it can be placed at rest that is not nearer the *hole*.

If a ball when placed comes to rest on the spot on which it is placed, and it subsequently *moves*, there is no penalty and the ball must be played as it lies, unless the provisions of any other *Rule* apply.

PENALTY FOR BREACH OF RULE 20-1, 20-2 OR 20-3:
Match play – Loss of hole; Stroke play – Two strokes.

20-4. WHEN BALL DROPPED OR PLACED IS IN PLAY

If the player's *ball in play* has been lifted, it is again in play when dropped or placed.

A *substituted ball* becomes the *ball in play* when it has been dropped or placed.

(Ball incorrectly substituted – see Rule 15-2)

(Lifting ball incorrectly substituted, dropped or placed – see Rule 20-6)

20-5. MAKING NEXT STROKE FROM WHERE PREVIOUS STROKE MADE

When a player elects or is required to make his next *stroke* from where a previous *stroke* was made, he must proceed as follows:

(a) On the Teeing Ground: The ball to be played must be played from within the *teeing ground*. It may be played from anywhere within the *teeing ground* and may be teed.

(b) Through the Green and in a Hazard: The ball to be played must be dropped.

(c) On the Putting Green: The ball to be played must be placed.

PENALTY FOR BREACH OF RULE 20-5:

Match play – Loss of hole; Stroke play – Two strokes.

20-6. LIFTING BALL INCORRECTLY SUBSTITUTED, DROPPED OR PLACED

A ball incorrectly *substituted*, dropped or placed in a wrong place or otherwise not in accordance with the *Rules* but not played may be lifted, without penalty, and the player must then proceed correctly.

20-7. PLAYING FROM WRONG PLACE
a. General

A player has played from a wrong place if he makes a *stroke* with his *ball in play*:

(i)   on a part of the *course* where the *Rules* do not permit a *stroke* to be played or a ball to be dropped or placed; or

(ii)   when the *Rules* require a dropped ball to be re-dropped or a *moved* ball to be replaced.

Note: For a ball played from outside the *teeing ground* or from a wrong *teeing ground* – see Rule 11-4.

b. Match Play

If a player makes a *stroke* from a wrong place, **he loses the hole**.

c. Stroke Play

If a *competitor* makes a *stroke* from a wrong place, **he incurs a penalty of two strokes under the applicable *Rule***. He must play out the hole with the ball played from the wrong place, without correcting his error, provided he has not committed a serious breach (see Note 1).

If a *competitor* becomes aware that he has played from a wrong place and believes that he may have committed a serious breach, he must, before making a *stroke* on the next *teeing ground*, play out the hole with a second ball dropped or placed in accordance with the *Rules*. If the hole being played is the last hole of the round, he must declare, before leaving the *putting green*, that he will play out the hole with a second ball dropped or placed in accordance with the *Rules*.

The *competitor* must report the facts to the *Committee* before returning his score card; if he fails to do so, **he is disqualified**. The *Committee* must determine whether the *competitor* has committed a serious breach of the applicable *Rule*. If he has, the score with the second ball counts and **the *competitor* must add two penalty strokes** to his score with that ball. If the *competitor* has committed a serious breach and has failed to correct it as outlined above, **he is disqualified**.

Note 1: A *competitor* is deemed to have committed a serious breach of the applicable *Rule* if the *Committee* considers he has gained a significant advantage as a result of playing from a wrong place.

Note 2: If a *competitor* plays a second ball under Rule 20-7c and it is ruled not to count, *strokes* made with that ball and *penalty strokes* incurred solely by playing that ball are disregarded. If the second ball is ruled to count, the

PLAYING FROM WRONG PLACE

If a player moves his ball-marker a putter head length to one side, he must remember to put it back before he putts. Otherwise, the player will be penalized for playing from a wrong place.

stroke made from the wrong place and any *strokes* subsequently taken with the original ball including *penalty strokes* incurred solely by playing that ball are disregarded.

RULE 20 INCIDENTS

Determining the exact moment at which a ball has been put into play was precisely defined on the 16th hole of the 2002 Bay Hill Invitational.

Reasonable evidence existed that Jeff Maggert's second shot at the par-5 finished in the water hazard in front of the green. After some searching, Maggert went back to a drop zone that was offered as an alternative for putting a ball back into play under the water hazard rule.

Searching continued as Maggert prepared to drop. Between the water and the putting green and slightly to the left was a bunker with enough of a lip as to make it impossible to see a ball lying just inside the lip on the water's side of the bunker if you were looking from the water side of the bunker, which was where the search had been taking place. A caddie up on the green, however, was looking back at the bunker with an unobstructed view under the water side bunker lip.

Just as Maggert released a ball in the drop zone, as it was falling to the ground from his hand, the caddie on the green yelled, "Here's a ball in the bunker." Because the two actions were nearly simultaneous, there was some confusion about whether or not Maggert could play his original ball.

The Rules official with Maggert explained that another ball had been put into play when he dropped the second ball in the drop zone, and the original ball was, therefore, lost. [Decision 27-1/2.]

With only two holes left in the round, and still doubtful of his rights under the Rules, Maggert asked if he could play both balls, use the score with his original ball if permitted, and get a final decision from the Committee when the round was finished. [Rule 3-3.] The Rules official assured him that was permitted. Both balls were played.

The Committee determined that the dropped ball was the ball in play from the instant that it left the player's hand. Therefore, the score with the dropped ball was the score for the hole.

At the 1984 Masters Tournament, Billy Casper was unaware or had momentarily forgotten that the method described in the Rules of Golf for dropping a ball had been changed that year. Casper used the old method, in which the player dropped over the shoulder, played ball and was assessed one penalty stroke.

Casper had won the tournament in 1970 after a playoff with Gene Littler. As a past champion, he was part of the 1984 field. The penalty he incurred in 1984 had no appreciable effect on the tournament results or prize money awarded. Had he dropped properly, Casper would still have missed the cut.

On the first green at the Olympic Club, during the first round of the U.S. Open, Mike Reid was replacing his ball when it slipped out of his hand. The ball fell onto and moved the coin that was marking its position. Reid inquired of the Rules official walking with the group and was told a penalty had not been incurred because the official believed Reid's

RELIEF SITUATIONS AND PROCEDURE

action was "directly attributable" to the act of replacing his ball. Reid finished the round, returned his scorecard, and went to the locker room.

When the incident was brought to the attention of senior Rules officials, it was determined that Reid's action was not "directly attributable to the specific act" of replacing his ball and that one penalty stroke should be added to his score, as stipulated by Rules 20-1 and 18-2. Reid was not disqualified for returning a score lower than he had actually made because the official walking with his group had initially told him there was no penalty.

Because of this incident, the phrase "directly attributable to the specific act" is now defined by Decision 20-1/15 and eliminates from consideration "accidental movement of the ball or the ball-marker which occurs before or after this specific act, such as dropping the ball or ball-marker, regardless of the height from which it was dropped…"

The infraction for lifting an opponent's ball without authorization can be deadly in match play. In the 1988 U.S. Amateur Championship, which was played at The Cascades in Hot Springs, Virginia, Danny Yates mistook his opponent's ball for his own and lifted it without permission. The mistake took place on the 21st hole of the 36-hole final round. The one-stroke penalty under Rule 18-3b resulted in Yates losing the hole to Eric Meeks, who eventually won the match, 7 and 6, and the championship.

Hale Irwin learned at the 1995 Senior Tour Championship that trying to do the right thing by correcting an error can sometimes compound the infraction and the resulting penalty.

At the Dunes Club in Myrtle Beach, Irwin erroneously replaced his ball on the 16th putting green in front of his fellow-competitor's marker. After putting, Irwin realized his mistake and, believing that he could correct his error, lifted his ball, replaced it in front of his marker and finished the hole from there.

His penalty was four strokes. When Irwin replaced his ball in front of his fellow-competitor's marker and putted, he played from a wrong place and incurred the two-stroke penalty under Rule 16-1b. When he subsequently lifted his ball from where it lay without marking its position and did not replace it, he also incurred the general penalty of two strokes under Rule 20-1.

RULE **21** CLEANING BALL

See **incident** involving Rule 21 on page 91

DEFINITIONS All defined terms are in *italics* and are listed alphabetically in the Definitions section – see pages 6–15.

A ball on the *putting green* may be cleaned when lifted under Rule 16-1b. Elsewhere, a ball may be cleaned when lifted except when it has been lifted:
a. To determine if it is unfit for play (Rule 5-3);
b. For identification (Rule 12-2), in which case it may be cleaned only to the extent necessary for identification; or
c. Because it is assisting or interfering with play (Rule 22).

If a player cleans his ball during play of a hole except as provided in this Rule, **he incurs a penalty of one stroke** and the ball, if lifted, must be replaced.

If a player who is required to replace a ball fails to do so, **he incurs the penalty** for breach of Rule 20-3a, but there is no additional penalty under Rule 21.

Exception: If a player incurs a penalty for failing to act in accordance with Rule 5-3, 12-2 or 22, there is no additional penalty under Rule 21.

RULE 21 INCIDENT

During the 1999 U.S. Open at Pinehurst Scott Hoch holed his bunker shot at the par-4 12th. During the clamor, the walking Rules official looked up to see two senior Rules officials motioning him to come over.

The senior officials reported that a spectator had alleged that Hoch's ball was mistakenly cleaned when lifted for interference at the 6th hole. Rule 22 permits the lifting of a ball that interferes with or assists the play of another player. Under such circumstances, except on the putting green, the ball may not be cleaned when lifted under Rule 22.

The senior officials asked the walking official if he could confirm whether Hoch's ball had been cleaned when lifted from the greenside rough. The walking official stated that his attention had been primarily focused on the lifting and replacing procedures and he was unaware of any cleaning violation.

It was decided to ask Hoch after he finished the round but before he returned his score card. When the inquiry was made Hoch replied that he did not recall since the incident had occurred two hours before. Hoch's caddie also said he did not recall. Parnevik and Jones, his playing partner, said they were not watching and could not say.

Since there was no evidence to the contrary, Hoch was found to have acted properly and he began the second round just four shots out of the lead.

RULE 22
BALL ASSISTING OR INTERFERING WITH PLAY

DEFINITIONS

All defined terms are in *italics* and are listed alphabetically in the Definitions section – see pages 6–15.

22-1. BALL ASSISTING PLAY

Except when a ball is in motion, if a player considers that a ball might assist any other player, he may:

a. lift the ball if it is his ball; or

b. have any other ball lifted.

A ball lifted under this Rule must be replaced (see Rule 20-3). The ball must not be cleaned unless it lies on the *putting green* (see Rule 21).

In stroke play, a player required to lift his ball may play first rather than lift the ball.

91

In stroke play, if the *Committee* determines that *competitors* have agreed not to lift a ball that might assist any other player, **they are disqualified**.

22-2. BALL INTERFERING WITH PLAY

See **incident** involving Rule 22-2 on pages 92–93

Except when a ball is in motion, if a player considers that the ball of another player might interfere with his play, he may have it lifted.

A ball lifted under this Rule must be replaced (see Rule 20-3). The ball must not be cleaned unless it lies on the *putting green* (see Rule 21).

In stroke play, a player required to lift his ball may play first rather than lift the ball.

Note: Except on the *putting green*, a player may not lift his ball solely because he considers that it might interfere with the play of another player. If a player lifts his ball without being asked to do so, **he incurs a penalty of one stroke** for a breach of Rule 18-2a, but there is no additional penalty under Rule 22.

PENALTY FOR BREACH OF RULE:
Match play – Loss of hole; Stroke play – Two strokes.

RULE 22 INCIDENTS

In a playoff situation, the general penalties in stroke or match play, can magnify the effect of the slightest infraction and invert apparent success to certain defeat or elimination.

All USGA match play championships begin with 36 holes of stroke play qualifying. The low 64 players comprise the resulting match play field. Stroke play qualifying for the 2002 U.S. Mid-Amateur Championship was comprised of one round at Round Hill Club and another at The Stanwich Club in Greenwich, Connecticut. At the conclusion of those 36 holes, twelve players were tied for the last seven places in the 64-man field. To resolve the tie, a stroke play playoff was held, beginning at Stanwich's 10th hole.

Standard procedure calls for all twelve players to complete the first playoff hole, determine who may or may not have been eliminated, and then play the next hole, and so on. Four players were eliminated on the tenth hole by scoring higher than the others. Eight competitors moved to the next tee still competing for seven spots.

The first group drove well and then played their approach shots to the par-4's putting green. One player's ball finished on the fringe in a position where it interfered with another's anticipated play from 20 yards short of the green. The player approaching from the fairway asked that the interfering ball on the fringe be lifted. [Rule 22.]

Under the Rules, a player may always have any other ball lifted if he considers that the ball might interfere with his play or assist the play of any other player. Under the note to Rule 22, it is specifically states that a ball "may not be cleaned when lifted under this Rule."

As you have read in several of the Rules incidents herein, the heat and distraction of competition sometimes obfuscate what would normally be second nature to a seasoned competitor. Other than on a putting green, when a ball is lifted under Rule 22, it is best that it be done carefully and in full view, so there is no question as to whether or not the ball has been cleaned on purpose or by accident. To avoid "the appearance of evil," as a noted Rules authority once put it, some competitors prefer to use only their thumb and forefinger to lift the ball, and then set it on the ground to the side. Others will hold the ball to their side, in full view, using only their thumb and forefinger.

At Stanwich, the player who lifted his ball was so absorbed by the demands of his impending shot and the result of the playoff that the restrictions under Rule 22 were apparently not in his mind. Thoughtlessly, he rolled his ball, which he had lifted from the fringe, in the palm of his hand cleaning it. Had the ball been on the green, there would have been no penalty for cleaning it.

The Rules Official with the group watched with dismay from his position in the fairway unable to prevent what had already taken place. He approached the player and asked, "Did you clean your ball?"

"Oh, I'm dead," responded the player realizing instantly what he had done unintentionally. Everyone was in shock at the unfortunate but unavoidable one stroke penalty that had to be levied.

The player took three more from the fringe for a double bogey six. The others in his group made fours and fives, as did those in the second playoff group. As the single high man for the hole, the infracting player was eliminated from the playoff. The field of 64 was established. Instead of continuing into the match play rounds, he was heading for home.

RULE **23** | LOOSE IMPEDIMENTS

DEFINITIONS

See **incident** involving Rule 23-1 on page 95

All defined terms are in *italics* and are listed alphabetically in the Definitions section – see pages 6–15.

23-1. RELIEF

Except when both the *loose impediment* and the ball lie in or touch the same *hazard*, any *loose impediment* may be removed without penalty.

If the ball lies anywhere other than on the *putting green* and the removal of a *loose impediment* by the player causes the ball to *move*, Rule 18-2a applies.

On the *putting green*, if the ball or ball-marker *moves* in the process of the player removing any *loose impediment*, the ball or ball-marker must be replaced. There is no penalty provided the movement of the ball or ball-marker is directly attributable to the removal of the *loose impediment*. Otherwise, if the player causes the ball to *move*, **he incurs a penalty of one stroke** under Rule 18-2a.

When a ball is in motion, a *loose impediment* that might influence the

A player is entitled to remove any loose impediment without penalty, except when both the loose impediment and the player's ball lie in or touch the same hazard.

Loose impediments are natural objects that come in all shapes and sizes. At the 1999 Phoenix Open, Tiger Woods learned that a player can receive assistance in removing a large loose impediment. Details of the incident can be reviewed on page 95.

movement of the ball must not be removed.

Note: If the ball lies in a *hazard*, the player must not touch or move any *loose impediment* lying in or touching the same *hazard* – see Rule 13-4c.

PENALTY FOR BREACH OF RULE:

Match play – Loss of hole; Stroke play – Two strokes.

(Searching for ball in *hazard* – see Rule 12-1)

(Touching *line of putt* – see Rule 16-1a)

RULE 23 INCIDENT

The Rules of Golf permitted Tiger Woods to gain assistance from his substantial gallery in moving a loose impediment during the 1999 Phoenix Open.

During the final round, Woods' drive from the 13th tee traveled 360 yards before finishing in the desert just off the left side of the fairway. The ball stopped about two feet directly behind a boulder that was roughly four feet wide, two feet high and two feet thick. The rock was too heavy for Woods to move by himself, and his ball was too close to it to play over or around. Without moving the rock, his best option would have been to play sideways into the fairway.

With 225 yards to the putting green, Woods was not inclined to pitch out without first knowing what his options were with regard to the rock.

PGA Tour Rules Official Orlando Pope appeared at the scene. With a glimmer of a smile on his face, Woods kicked the rock and asked, "… It's not a pebble but is it a loose impediment?"

The definition within the Rules of Golf states that loose impediments are natural objects that are not fixed or growing, not solidly embedded and do not adhere to the ball. There is no reference to size or weight.

Decision 23-1/2 states that stones of any size are loose impediments and may be removed, as long as they are not solidly embedded and their removal does not unduly delay play.

Pope replied, "It's readily movable if you have people who can move it real quick."

"Really?" Woods responded to the revelation quietly.

Then Pope added in an inquiring tone, "But it kind of looks embedded to me."

"It's embedded?" Woods asked as they both stepped back to look.

Pope decided the stone was just lying on the desert floor and was not solidly embedded. He also knew that Decision 23-1/3 specifically permits spectators, caddies, fellow-competitors, essentially anyone to assist in removing a large loose impediment.

Several men rolled the stone out of Woods' line of play as others watched and cheered. Following the removal, Woods shook each man's hand and then played his shot directly toward the green, where it finished in the right greenside bunker.

Golf's stars have always enjoyed and suffered the effects of their large galleries. Bobby Jones had to be protected by Marines when he completed his Grand Slam at Merion in 1930. Sam Snead, Arnold Palmer and Jack Nicklaus often had errant shots stopped by those who followed them.

95

In addition to the times they were helped, imagine the number of times that Jones, Snead, Palmer, Nicklaus and Woods have been distracted by a movement or noise coming from the galleries, photographers, reporters and security officers that follow them. It has never been the function of the Rules of Golf to try to equalize these varied possibilities.

RULE **24** OBSTRUCTIONS

DEFINITIONS

All defined terms are in *italics* and are listed alphabetically in the Definitions section – see pages 6–15.

See **incident** involving Rule 24-1 on page 102–103

24-1. MOVABLE OBSTRUCTION

A player may take relief without penalty from a movable *obstruction* as follows:

a. If the ball does not lie in or on the *obstruction*, the *obstruction* may be removed. If the ball *moves*, it must be replaced, and there is no penalty provided that the movement of the ball is directly attributable to the removal of the *obstruction*. Otherwise, Rule 18-2a applies.

b. If the ball lies in or on the *obstruction*, the ball may be lifted, and the *obstruction* removed. The ball must *through the green* or in a *hazard* be dropped, or on the *putting green* be placed, as near as possible to the spot directly under the place where the ball lay in or on the *obstruction*, but not nearer the *hole*.

The ball may be cleaned when lifted under this Rule.

When a ball is in motion, an *obstruction* that might influence the

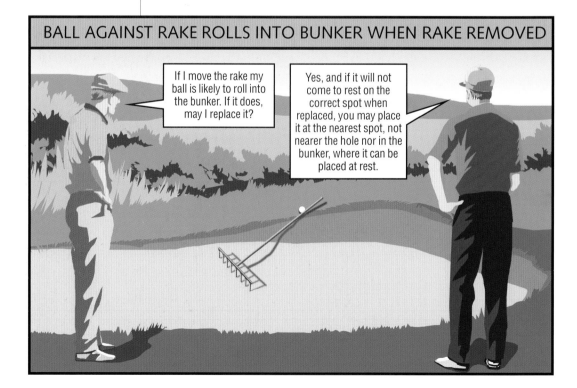

BALL AGAINST RAKE ROLLS INTO BUNKER WHEN RAKE REMOVED

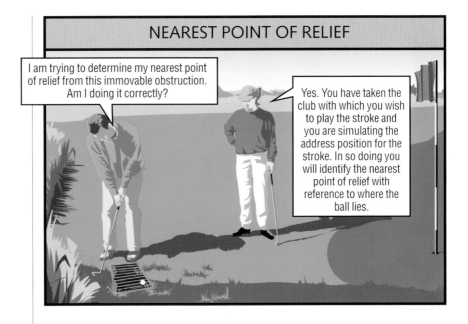

movement of the ball, other than an attended *flagstick* or *equipment* of the players, must not be removed.

(Exerting influence on ball – see Rule 1-2)

Note: If a ball to be dropped or placed under this Rule is not immediately recoverable, another ball may be *substituted*.

24-2. IMMOVABLE OBSTRUCTION

a. Interference

See **incidents** involving Rule 24-2 on page 102–103

Interference by an immovable *obstruction* occurs when a ball lies in or on the *obstruction*, or when the *obstruction* interferes with the player's *stance* or the area of his intended swing. If the player's ball lies on the *putting green*, interference also occurs if an immovable *obstruction* on the *putting green* intervenes on his *line of putt*. Otherwise, intervention on the *line of play* is not, of itself, interference under this Rule.

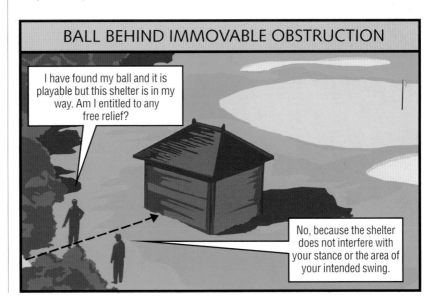

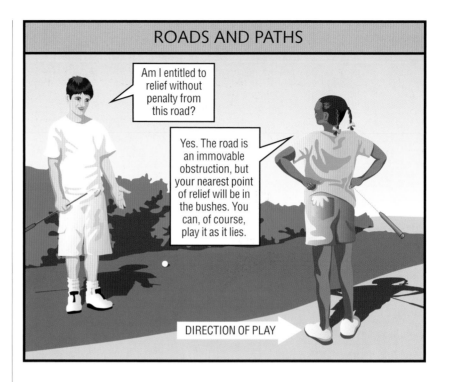

b. Relief

Except when the ball is in a *water hazard* or a *lateral water hazard*, a player may take relief from interference by an immovable *obstruction* as follows:

(i) **Through the Green:** If the ball lies *through the green*, the player must lift the ball and drop it without penalty within one club-length of and not nearer the *hole* than the *nearest point of relief*. The *nearest point*

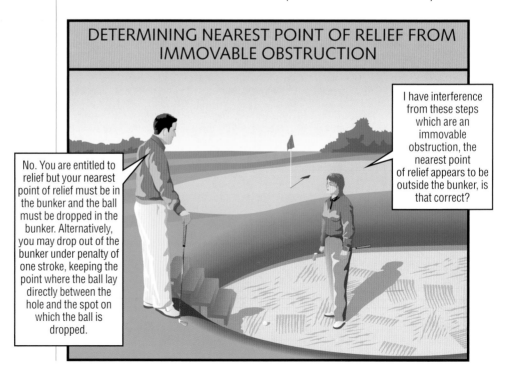

of relief must not be in a *hazard* or on a *putting green*. When the ball is dropped within one club-length of the *nearest point of relief*, the ball must first strike a part of the *course* at a spot that avoids interference by the immovable *obstruction* and is not in a *hazard* and not on a *putting green*.

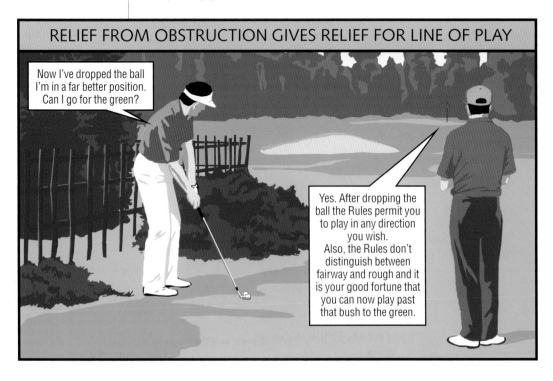

(ii) **In a Bunker:** If the ball is in a *bunker*, the player must lift the ball and drop it either:

(a) Without penalty, in accordance with Clause (i) above, except that the *nearest point of relief* must be in the *bunker* and the ball must be dropped in the *bunker*; or

(b) **Under penalty of one stroke**, outside the *bunker* keeping the point where the ball lay directly between the *hole* and the spot on which the ball is dropped, with no limit to how far behind the *bunker* the ball may be dropped.

(iii) **On the Putting Green:** If the ball lies on the *putting green*, the player must lift the ball and place it without penalty at the *nearest point of relief* that is not in a *hazard*. The *nearest point of relief* may be off the *putting green*.

(iv) **On the Teeing Ground:** If the ball lies on the *teeing ground*, the player must lift the ball and drop it without penalty in accordance with Clause (i) above.

The ball may be cleaned when lifted under this Rule.

(Ball rolling to a position where there is interference by the condition from which relief was taken – see Rule 20-2c(v)

Exception: A player may not take relief under this Rule if (a) it is clearly unreasonable for him to make a *stroke* because of interference by anything other than an immovable *obstruction* or (b) interference by an immovable *obstruction* would occur only through use of an unnecessarily abnormal *stance*, swing or direction of play.

Note 1: If a ball is in a *water hazard* (including a *lateral water hazard*), the player may not take relief from interference by an immovable *obstruction*. The player must play the ball as it lies or proceed under Rule 26-1.

Note 2: If a ball to be dropped or placed under this Rule is not immediately recoverable, another ball may be *substituted*.

Note 3: The *Committee* may make a Local Rule stating that the player must determine the *nearest point of relief* without crossing over, through or under the *obstruction*.

24-3. BALL LOST IN OBSTRUCTION

It is a question of fact whether a ball *lost* after having been struck toward an *obstruction* is *lost* in the *obstruction*. In order to treat the ball as *lost* in the *obstruction*, there must be reasonable evidence to that effect. In the absence of such evidence, the ball must be treated as a *lost ball* and Rule 27 applies.

a. Ball Lost in Movable Obstruction

If a ball is *lost* in a movable *obstruction*, a player may, without penalty, remove the *obstruction* and must *through the green* or in a *hazard* drop a ball, or on the *putting green* place a ball, as near as possible to the spot directly under the place where the ball last crossed the outermost limits of the movable *obstruction*, but not nearer the *hole*.

b. Ball Lost in Immovable Obstruction

If a ball is *lost* in an immovable *obstruction*, the spot where the ball last

crossed the outermost limits of the *obstruction* must be determined and, for the purpose of applying this Rule, the ball is deemed to lie at this spot and the player may take relief as follows:

(i) **Through the Green:** If the ball last crossed the outermost limits of the immovable *obstruction* at a spot *through the green*, the player may *substitute* another ball without penalty and take relief as prescribed in Rule 24-2b(i).

(ii) **In a Bunker:** If the ball last crossed the outermost limits of the immovable *obstruction* at a spot in a *bunker*, the player may *substitute* another ball without penalty and take relief as prescribed in Rule 24-2b(ii).

(iii) **In a Water Hazard (including a Lateral Water Hazard):** If the ball last crossed the outermost limits of the immovable *obstruction* at a spot in a *water hazard*, the player is not entitled to relief without penalty. The player must proceed under Rule 26-1.

(iv) **On the Putting Green:** If the ball last crossed the outermost limits of the immovable *obstruction* at a spot on the *putting green*, the player may *substitute* another ball without penalty and take relief as prescribed in Rule 24-2b(iii).

PENALTY FOR BREACH OF RULE:
Match play – Loss of hole; Stroke play – Two strokes.

101

RULE 24 INCIDENTS

The basic tenets of the Rules, as they have developed during the past 260 years, have been to play the course as you find it, the ball as it lies, and, if you are unsure of the proper procedure, to do what is fair.

Playing the course as he found it put Tom Purtzer on the clubhouse roof at the 2003 U.S. Senior Open. By definition, a clubhouse is an obstruction from which free relief is granted unless it is out of bounds or has been declared an integral part of the course. Often the clubhouse is marked as out of bounds because it lies so near the line of play - behind the final green for instance - and free relief would be inappropriate. At Inverness in Toledo, Ohio, the clubhouse was built a good distance to the right of the final hole. It is part of the golf course, although far enough to the side so as not generally considered an obstacle that would have to be negotiated in the normal course of play. National championships, however, have a tendency to produce unusual Rules situations.

During the second round, Tom Purtzer was playing the 18th hole, it was his ninth hole of the day because the group had started at the 10th, and his drive had finished in the right rough. Roughly 100 yards from the green, Purtzer made his second shot that was described by onlookers as a "high shank." The ball was so high and so right that it landed on the flat part of the clubhouse roof.

Wrongly assuming the clubhouse to be out of bounds, Purtzer was preparing to drop a second ball, under Rule 27, take a penalty stroke and play again from the rough. However, before he dropped the second ball, he was stopped by the walking Rules Official and told the clubhouse was not out of bounds, but rather an obstruction. This was verified over the radio, and Purtzer was given his options under Rule 24-3.

While it was within Purtzer's rights to climb to the roof, search five minutes for his ball and, if found, play it from that place [within the obstruction], there was reasonable evidence that the ball was lost in the obstruction. Therefore, having determined where the ball last crossed the outer limits of the obstruction, he was entitled to substitute a ball and proceed under the provisions of Rule 24-3b.

During the second round of the 1949 British Open, Harry Bradshaw was faithful to the tenet of doing what seems fair when you are unsure as to how to proceed. Having shot a stunning first round 68 over Royal St. George's on the southeast coast of England, Bradshaw was tied with Roberto De Vicenzo one stroke behind Jimmy Adams. Playing the 5th hole, Bradshaw's ball rolled into a beer bottle with a broken neck lying in the rough.

Rather than requesting a ruling for the relief to which he was entitled, Bradshaw determined on his own that he must play the ball as it lay. He took out his sand wedge and made a swing shattering the bottle and moving the ball slightly forward. His score for the hole was a double bogey six.

The result of his playing out of this movable obstruction was that Bradshaw ultimately tied Bobby Locke of South Africa at 283. In the resulting 36-hole playoff, Locke bested Bradshaw, 136 to 147, to win the first of Locke's four British Open Championships.

Under Rule 24-1, because Bradshaw's ball was in a movable obstruction, the ball could have been lifted and cleaned without penalty, the bottle removed, and the ball dropped as nearly as possible to the spot directly under the place where the ball lay when it was in the bottle.

In choosing to take relief from an immovable obstruction, the ball must be dropped in a place that avoids interference by the immovable obstruction. Full relief must be taken. Payne Stewart learned this detail in 1993 during the PGA Tour's annual stop in San Diego.

Taking relief from a cart path, Stewart dropped his ball in a place where, after taking his stance, the heel of his right shoe was still on the obstructing cart path. The television broadcast showed the infraction clearly, and Stewart was penalized two strokes for not taking complete relief from the immovable obstruction. [Rule 24-2.]

When the Committee declares an obstruction to be an integral part of the golf course, it eliminates the option for free relief because, by definition, the object or building is no longer considered an obstruction under the Rules. It is considered to be no different than a tree or a blade of grass. The most famous example of this is the Road Hole at the Old Course in St. Andrews. When a ball lies upon this road immediately to the right of the green, it must be played as it lies. As the hole's name signals, the road has always been the most important element of the 17th hole, and to afford free relief would eliminate one of the hole's essential obstacles. Thus, it is an integral part of the golf course.

When the Committee declares an immovable obstruction to be an integral part of the course, in this case the road behind the 17th green of the Old Course at St Andrews, relief without penalty is not available.

RULE **25**

ABNORMAL GROUND CONDITIONS, EMBEDDED BALL AND WRONG PUTTING GREEN

DEFINITIONS

All defined terms are in *italics* and are listed alphabetically in the Definitions section – see pages 6–15.

25-1. ABNORMAL GROUND CONDITIONS
a. Interference

Interference by an *abnormal ground condition* occurs when a ball lies in or touches the condition or when the condition interferes with the player's *stance* or the area of his intended swing. If the player's ball lies on the *putting green*, interference also occurs if an *abnormal ground condition* on the *putting green* intervenes on his *line of putt*. Otherwise, intervention

A rut made by a tractor is not ground under repair, but the Committee would be justified in declaring a deep rut to be ground under repair.

A fallen tree still attached to its stump is not ground under repair, but it can be so declared by the Committee.

on the *line of play* is not, of itself, interference under this *Rule*.

Note: The *Committee* may make a Local Rule denying the player relief from interference with his *stance* by an *abnormal ground condition*.

b. Relief

See **incident** involving Rule 25-1b on page 111

Except when the ball is in a *water hazard* or a *lateral water hazard*, a player may take relief from interference by an *abnormal ground condition* as follows:

(i)   **Through the Green:** If the ball lies *through the green*, the player must lift the ball and drop it without penalty within one club-length of and not nearer the *hole* than the *nearest point of relief*. The *nearest point of relief* must not be in a *hazard* or on a *putting green*. When the ball is dropped within one club-length of the *nearest point of relief*, the ball must first strike a part of the *course* at a spot that avoids interference by the condition and is not in a *hazard* and not on a *putting green*.

(ii) **In a Bunker:** If the ball is in a *bunker*, the player must lift the ball and drop it either:

(a) Without penalty, in accordance with Clause (i) above, except that the *nearest point of relief* must be in the *bunker* and the ball must be dropped in the *bunker*, or if complete relief is impossible, as near as possible to the spot where the ball lay, but not nearer the *hole*, on a part of the *course* in the *bunker* that affords maximum available relief from the condition; or

(b) **Under penalty of one stroke**, outside the *bunker* keeping the point where the ball lay directly between the *hole* and the spot on which the ball is dropped, with no limit to how far behind the *bunker* the ball may be dropped.

(iii) **On the Putting Green:** If the ball lies on the *putting green*, the player must lift the ball and place it without penalty at the *nearest point of*

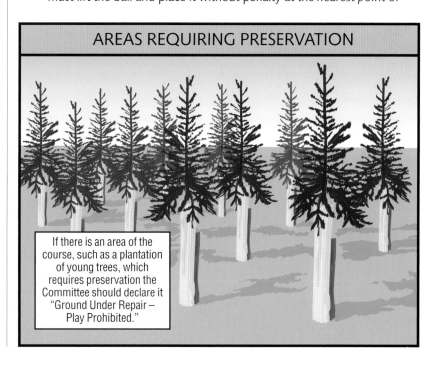

AREAS REQUIRING PRESERVATION

If there is an area of the course, such as a plantation of young trees, which requires preservation the Committee should declare it "Ground Under Repair – Play Prohibited."

CASUAL WATER ON PUTTING GREEN

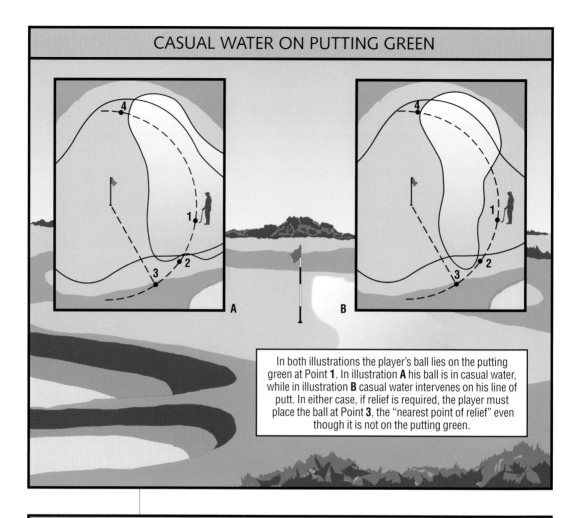

In both illustrations the player's ball lies on the putting green at Point **1**. In illustration **A** his ball is in casual water, while in illustration **B** casual water intervenes on his line of putt. In either case, if relief is required, the player must place the ball at Point **3**, the "nearest point of relief" even though it is not on the putting green.

BALL CLOSE TO CASUAL WATER: LEFT HANDED STROKE NOT REASONABLE

BALL CLOSE TO CASUAL WATER: LEFT HANDED STROKE REASONABLE

A player who can't play a normal right-handed stroke because of a tree, may decide to play left-handed, in which case he would be standing in casual water.

Direction of play

She is entitled to relief from the casual water for a left-handed stroke and having dropped the ball, she may then play right-handed or left-handed.

BALL IN CASUAL WATER IN BUNKER

I am taking relief from this casual water. Must I drop the ball at the nearest point of relief or may I drop it within one club-length of the nearest point of relief not nearer the hole.

As you are able to take complete relief from the casual water, you are allowed to drop within one club-length of the nearest point of relief. However, if complete relief had been impossible and you were taking maximum available relief, the ball would have to be dropped on the spot which gave maximum available relief.

relief that is not in a *hazard*, or if complete relief is impossible, at the nearest position to where it lay that affords maximum available relief from the condition, but not nearer the *hole* and not in a *hazard*. The *nearest point of relief* or maximum available relief may be off the *putting green*.

(iv) **On the Teeing Ground:** If the ball lies on the *teeing ground*, the player must lift the ball and drop it without penalty in accordance with Clause (i) above.

The ball may be cleaned when lifted under Rule 25-1b.

(Ball rolling to a position where there is interference by the condition from which relief was taken – see Rule 20-2c(v))

Exception: A player may not take relief under this Rule if (a) it is clearly unreasonable for him to make a *stroke* because of interference by anything other than an *abnormal ground condition* or (b) interference by an *abnormal ground condition* would occur only through use of an unnecessarily abnormal *stance*, swing or direction of play.

Note 1: If a ball is in a *water hazard* (including a *lateral water hazard*), the player is not entitled to relief without penalty from interference by an *abnormal ground condition*. The player must play the ball as it lies (unless prohibited by Local Rule) or proceed under Rule 26-1.

Note 2: If a ball to be dropped or placed under this Rule is not immediately recoverable, another ball may be *substituted*.

c. Ball Lost

See **incident** involving Rule 25-1c on page 111

It is a question of fact whether a ball *lost* after having been struck toward an *abnormal ground condition* is *lost* in such condition. In order to treat the ball as *lost* in the *abnormal ground condition*, there must be reasonable evidence to that effect. In the absence of such evidence, the ball must be treated as a *lost ball* and Rule 27 applies.

If a ball is *lost* in an *abnormal ground condition*, the spot where the ball last crossed the outermost limits of the condition must be determined and, for the purpose of applying this Rule, the ball is deemed to lie at this spot and the player may take relief as follows:

(i) **Through the Green:** If the ball last crossed the outermost limits of the *abnormal ground condition* at a spot *through the green*, the player may *substitute* another ball without penalty and take relief as prescribed in Rule 25-1b(i).

(ii) **In a Bunker:** If the ball last crossed the outermost limits of the *abnormal ground condition* at a spot in a *bunker*, the player may *substitute* another ball without penalty and take relief as prescribed in Rule 25-1b(ii).

(iii) **In a Water Hazard (including a Lateral Water Hazard):** If the ball last crossed the outermost limits of the *abnormal ground condition* at a spot in a *water hazard*, the player is not entitled to relief without penalty. The player must proceed under Rule 26-1.

(iv) **On the Putting Green:** If the ball last crossed the outermost limits of the *abnormal ground condition* at a spot on the *putting green*, the player may *substitute* another ball without penalty and take relief as prescribed in Rule 25-1b(iii).

25-2. EMBEDDED BALL

A ball embedded in its own pitch-mark in the ground in any closely mown area *through the green* may be lifted, cleaned and dropped, without penalty, as near as possible to the spot where it lay but not nearer the *hole*. The ball when dropped must first strike a part of the *course through the green*. "Closely mown area" means any area of the *course*, including paths through the rough, cut to fairway height or less.

25-3. WRONG PUTTING GREEN
a. Interference

Interference by a *wrong putting green* occurs when a ball is on the *wrong putting green*.

Interference to a player's *stance* or the area of his intended swing is not, of itself, interference under this Rule.

See **incident** involving Rule 25-3 on page 111–112

b. Relief

If a player's ball lies on a *wrong putting green*, he must not play the ball as it lies. He must take relief, without penalty, as follows:

The player must lift the ball and drop it within one club-length of and not nearer the hole than the *nearest point of relief*. The *nearest point of relief* must not be in a *hazard* or on a *putting green*. When dropping the ball within one club-length of the *nearest point of relief*, the ball must first strike a part of the *course* at a spot that avoids interference by the *wrong putting green* and is not in a *hazard* and not on a *putting green*. The ball may be cleaned when lifted under this Rule.

PENALTY FOR BREACH OF RULE:
Match play – Loss of hole; Stroke play – Two strokes.

RULE 25 INCIDENTS

Patty Sheehan was able to use Rule 25 to aid her in tying Juli Inkster during regulation play of the 1992 U.S. Women's Open. A sudden downpour across the hills of western Pennsylvania suspended play at Oakmont Country Club during the final round. Once play resumed, casual water was present in various places on the course.

At the final hole, Sheehan needed a birdie three to tie Inkster and force a playoff. Sheehan's drive was not promising. Her ball drifted to the right and settled in the high, wet rough.

Sheehan was faced with a mid-iron shot from wet, U.S. Women's Open rough that had to stop near the hole on an undulating green that is guarded front right and left by large bunkers.

Upon taking her stance water was visible that fell within the definition of casual water as "any temporary accumulation of water on the course which is visible before or after the player takes his stance and is not in a water hazard."

Though Sheehan's ball was off the fairway in the rough, the Rules of Golf make no distinction between rough and fairway as regards abnormal ground conditions. Directions for relief under Rule 25-1 state simply that if the ball lies through the green, the nearest point of relief shall be determined which is not in a hazard or on a putting green. Once that point is found, the player must drop the ball within one club-length and no nearer the hole.

In determining her nearest point of relief plus the one club-length, Sheehan discovered that her dropping point was in the fairway. Under the watchful eyes of a walking Rules official and an observer, she lifted the ball from the rough and appropriately dropped it in the fairway. Her second shot landed short of the putting green and ran onto the green. The ball finished close enough that Sheehan was able to make the birdie putt and tie Inkster after 72 holes.

In the following day's 18-hole playoff, Sheehan scored 72 to Inkster's 74 and won the first of her two U.S. Women's Open Championships.

During the second round of The Players Championship in 1999, marshals at the 18th green watched Greg Norman's ball roll into a hole made by a burrowing animal. When a ball is lost in an abnormal ground condition, there must be reasonable evidence to that effect. Suspecting that the ball might have gone into the burrowing animal hole is not good enough and, indeed, the Australian started to put his hand into the hole to determine if the ball was there.

The attending official told Norman that the marshals' statements that they had seen the ball go into the burrowing animal hole constituted reasonable evidence. Therefore, he was entitled to relief without penalty, and it was not necessary to reach into the hole in order to retrieve the ball.

A rare incidence of playing from a wrong putting green took place at the 1990 U.S. Senior Open at Ridgewood Country Club in Paramus, NJ.

Ridgewood has 27 holes. The third nine was out of play for the championship but not out of bounds. From the second tee, a player hooked his drive onto a green that is part of the third nine. From that green, the competitor played back to the second hole of the competitive course.

An observant marshal queried the player's procedure with a Rules official, and the player was penalized two strokes under Rule 25-3. It is important to note that had the player's ball been on the fringe of the putting green requiring a stance, by either foot, on the wrong putting green, the player would have been required to play the ball as it lay and would have incurred no penalty.

RULE **26** WATER HAZARDS (INCLUDING LATERAL WATER HAZARDS)

DEFINITIONS

All defined terms are in *italics* and are listed alphabetically in the Definitions section – see pages 6–15.

26-1. RELIEF FOR BALL IN WATER HAZARD

It is a question of fact whether a ball *lost* after having been struck toward a *water hazard* is *lost* inside or outside the *hazard*. In order to treat the ball as *lost* in the *hazard*, there must be reasonable evidence that the ball lodged in it. In the absence of such evidence, the ball must be treated as a *lost ball* and Rule 27 applies.

If a ball is in or is *lost* in a *water hazard* (whether the ball lies in water or not), the player may **under penalty of one stroke:**

a. Play a ball as nearly as possible at the spot from which the original ball was last played (see Rule 20-5); or

b. Drop a ball behind the *water hazard*, keeping the point at which the original ball last crossed the margin of the *water hazard* directly between the

See **incident** involving Rule 26-1b on page 116–117

Jean Van de Velde's difficulty with the Barry Burn at the 72nd hole of the 1999 British Open resulted in a three-way playoff for the championship. See the details of his unfortunate brush with Rule 26-1 in the incident on page 117.

REASONABLE EVIDENCE BALL IN WATER HAZARD

BALL CROSSING MARGIN OF WATER HAZARD

RELIEF FROM LATERAL WATER HAZARD

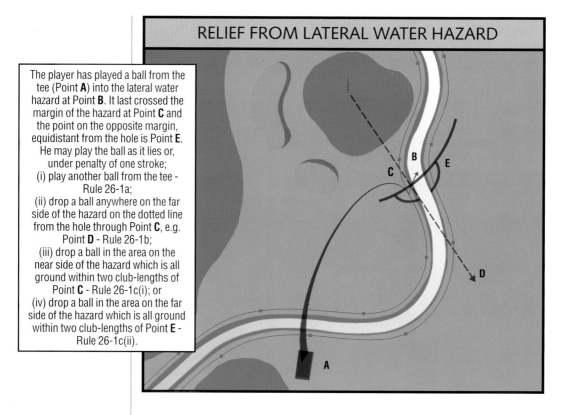

The player has played a ball from the tee (Point **A**) into the lateral water hazard at Point **B**. It last crossed the margin of the hazard at Point **C** and the point on the opposite margin, equidistant from the hole is Point **E**. He may play the ball as it lies or, under penalty of one stroke;
(i) play another ball from the tee - Rule 26-1a;
(ii) drop a ball anywhere on the far side of the hazard on the dotted line from the hole through Point **C**, e.g. Point **D** - Rule 26-1b;
(iii) drop a ball in the area on the near side of the hazard which is all ground within two club-lengths of Point **C** - Rule 26-1c(i); or
(iv) drop a ball in the area on the far side of the hazard which is all ground within two club-lengths of Point **E** - Rule 26-1c(ii).

hole and the spot on which the ball is dropped, with no limit to how far behind the *water hazard* the ball may be dropped; or

c. As additional options available only if the ball last crossed the margin of a *lateral water hazard*, drop a ball outside the *water hazard* within two club-lengths of and not nearer the *hole* than (i) the point where the original ball

BALL PLAYED FROM WITHIN WATER HAZARD

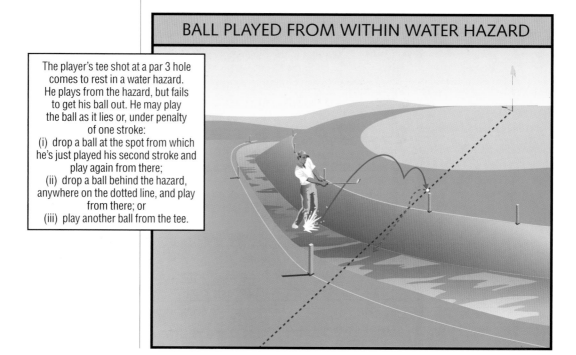

The player's tee shot at a par 3 hole comes to rest in a water hazard. He plays from the hazard, but fails to get his ball out. He may play the ball as it lies or, under penalty of one stroke:
(i) drop a ball at the spot from which he's just played his second stroke and play again from there;
(ii) drop a ball behind the hazard, anywhere on the dotted line, and play from there; or
(iii) play another ball from the tee.

Darren Clarke attempts to play his ball which lies in a lateral water hazard.
Lateral water hazards must be defined by red stakes or lines.

last crossed the margin of the *water hazard* or (ii) a point on the opposite margin of the *water hazard* equidistant from the *hole*.

The ball may be lifted and cleaned when proceeding under this Rule.
(Prohibited actions when ball is in a *hazard* – see Rule 13-4)
(Ball moving in water in a water *hazard* – see Rule 14-6)

26-2. BALL PLAYED WITHIN WATER HAZARD
a. Ball Comes to Rest in Same or Another Water Hazard
If a ball played from within a *water hazard* comes to rest in the same or another *water hazard* after the *stroke*, the player may:

(i)   proceed under Rule 26-1a. If, after dropping in the *hazard*, the player elects not to play the dropped ball, he may:

(a) with reference to this *hazard*, proceed under Rule 26-1b, or if applicable Rule 26-1c, adding the **additional penalty of one stroke** prescribed by that Rule; or

(b) **add an additional penalty of one stroke** and play a ball as nearly as possible at the spot from which the last *stroke* from outside a *water hazard* was made (see Rule 20-5); or

(ii)   proceed under Rule 26-1b, or if applicable Rule 26-1c; or

(iii)   **under penalty of one stroke**, play a ball as nearly as possible at the spot from which the last *stroke* from outside a *water hazard* was made (see Rule 20-5).

b. Ball Lost or Unplayable Outside Hazard or Out of Bounds

If a ball played from within a *water hazard* is *lost* or declared unplayable outside the *hazard* or is *out of bounds*, the player may, after taking a **penalty of one stroke** under Rule 27-1 or 28a:

(i)   play a ball as nearly as possible at the spot in the *hazard* from which the original ball was last made (see Rule 20-5); or

(ii)   proceed under Rule 26-1b, or if applicable Rule 26-1c, **adding the additional penalty of one stroke** prescribed by the Rule and using as the reference point the point where the original ball last crossed the margin of the *hazard* before it came to rest in the *hazard*; or

(iii)   **add an additional penalty of one stroke** and play a ball as nearly as possible at the spot from which the last *stroke* from outside the *hazard* was made (see Rule 20-5).

Note 1: When proceeding under Rule 26-2b, the player is not required to drop a ball under Rule 27-1 or 28a. If he does drop a ball, he is not required to play it. He may alternatively proceed under Rule 26-2b(ii) or (iii).

Note 2: If a ball played from within a *water hazard* is declared unplayable outside the *hazard*, nothing in Rule 26-2b precludes the player from proceeding under Rule 28b or c.

PENALTY FOR BREACH OF RULE:
Match play – Loss of hole; Stroke play – Two strokes.

RULE 26 INCIDENTS

Relief procedures under the Rules provide the mechanism for extricating yourself from difficult situations. Once the criteria for relief and any penalties have been applied, the clock is reset, so to speak, and play continues anew. The possibility of new Rules situations lie ahead.

On the 18th hole of the EMC World Cup at Vista Vallarta in Puerta Vallarta, Mexico, Thomas Levet could not have realized how quickly his water hazard penalty would repeat itself.

With his partner, Rafael Jacquelin, out of the hole and the French team leading by one, Levet played his approach from the fairway into a lateral water hazard to the front and left of the green. He chose to take relief under option c of Rule 26-1, and dropped a ball on the steep, closely mowed grass bank beside the water and the green where it came to rest. The ball was in play.

Gathering his wits, Levet took his time to look over his little pitch to the hole. He walked onto the green to assess what would be needed next. On his way back, his ball began to move and rolled back into the lateral water hazard from which he had taken relief.

Because the ball had been at rest after his taking relief, and because Levet had not addressed the ball or done anything to cause it to move, the ball was back in the hazard and could only be removed under penalty of an additional stroke. So, he was two in the hazard the first time, three out with the penalty, and then four out with a second penalty stroke under the water hazard rule. A new point of reference for where the ball last crossed the margin of the hazard had to be determined for the second drop.

Needless to say, Levet's fifth shot was played expeditiously.

The most remorseful Rule 26 incident of the past decade came at Carnoustie's 18th hole during the 1999 British Open. Jean Van de Velde needed only a double bogey to become the first Frenchman to win the championship since 1907.

A short time after playing from the tee, he was standing in the Barry Burn with his navy blue trousers rolled to his knees contemplating his fate and his options under Rule 26.

Having played a driver from the tee, the Frenchman's ball had finished well right but safely on a peninsula created by a bend in the burn. Instead of laying up with his second, Van de Velde attempted to play a 2-iron to the distant green. His shot was a bit wayward and it ricocheted off a grandstand railing, a stone wall and finally settled behind the second crossing of the burn in heavy rough.

Attempting to chop his ball out of the rough and over the burn, he instead chunked it badly and the ball finished in the shallow water of the burn. As the stream flows perpendicular to the line of play, it was marked with a yellow line indicating a water hazard - not the red line of a lateral water hazard.

As such, Van de Velde's options were three. He could play the ball without penalty as it lay. For a one-stroke penalty, he could play again from where he last played, or he could drop behind the hazard keeping the point at which his ball last crossed the margin of the hazard directly between the hole and the spot on which the ball would be dropped, with no limit to how far behind the hazard he might want to go.

Three in the water, and needing a six to win the British Open, the Frenchman contemplated playing out of the water in order to avoid the penalty stroke. To make such an assessment, he decided to step into the water to see what the shot required. Having removed his shoes and socks, Van de Velde rolled up his trouser legs and lowered himself down the stone wall into the shallow water.

Van de Velde was left standing alone in the dark water, wedge in hand, assessing his ability to play the submerged ball out of the hazard. After several minutes, discretion became the better part of valor and Van de Velde chose option b under Rule 26-1. He dropped a ball behind the hazard on the stipulated line, suffered a penalty stroke and played his fifth shot to the right greenside bunker. His up-and-down from the bunker resulted in a score of seven and a playoff between Paul Lawrie, Justin Leonard and Van de Velde, which Lawrie won.

RULE  **BALL LOST OR OUT OF BOUNDS; PROVISIONAL BALL**

DEFINITIONS All defined terms are in *italics* and are listed alphabetically in the Definitions section – see pages 6–15.

27-1. BALL LOST OR OUT OF BOUNDS

If a ball is *lost* or is *out of bounds*, the player must play a ball, **under penalty of one stroke**, as nearly as possible at the spot from which the original ball was last played (see Rule 20-5).

Exceptions:

1. If there is reasonable evidence that the original ball is *lost* in a *water hazard*, the player must proceed in accordance with Rule 26-1.

2. If there is reasonable evidence that the original ball is *lost* in an *obstruction* (Rule 24-3) or an *abnormal ground condition* (Rule 25-1c) the player may proceed under the applicable *Rule*.

PENALTY FOR BREACH OF RULE 27-1:
Match play – Loss of hole; Stroke play – Two strokes.

27-2. PROVISIONAL BALL
a. Procedure

See **incident** involving Rule 27-2 on page 121

If a ball may be *lost* outside a *water hazard* or may be *out of bounds*, to save time the player may play another ball provisionally in accordance with Rule 27-1. The player must inform his opponent in match play or his *marker* or a *fellow-competitor* in stroke play that he intends to play a *provisional ball*, and he must play it before he or his *partner* goes forward to search for the original ball.

  If he fails to do so and plays another ball, that ball is not a *provisional ball* and becomes the *ball in play* **under penalty of stroke and distance** (Rule 27-1); the original ball is *lost*.
(Order of play from *teeing ground* – see Rule 10-3)
Note: If a *provisional ball* played under Rule 27-2a might be *lost* outside a

BALL FOUND WITHIN FIVE MINUTES

PROVISIONAL BALL BECOMES BALL IN PLAY

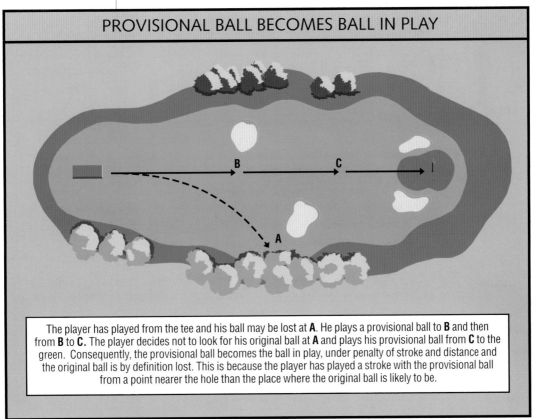

The player has played from the tee and his ball may be lost at **A**. He plays a provisional ball to **B** and then from **B** to **C**. The player decides not to look for his original ball at **A** and plays his provisional ball from **C** to the green. Consequently, the provisional ball becomes the ball in play, under penalty of stroke and distance and the original ball is by definition lost. This is because the player has played a stroke with the provisional ball from a point nearer the hole than the place where the original ball is likely to be.

PROVISIONAL BALL PLAYED: ORIGINAL BALL FOUND UNPLAYABLE

A player plays a provisional ball as his ball may be lost. The original ball is found within five minutes and before the provisional ball has become the ball in play, but the ball is unplayable. The player must abandon the provisional ball and proceed with the original ball.

water hazard or out of bounds, the player may play another *provisional ball*. If another *provisional ball* is played, it bears the same relationship to the previous *provisional ball* as the first *provisional ball* bears to the original ball.

b. When Provisional Ball Becomes Ball in Play

The player may play a *provisional ball* until he reaches the place where the original ball is likely to be. If he plays a *stroke* with the *provisional ball* from the place where the original ball is likely to be or from a point nearer the *hole* than that place, the original ball is *lost* and the *provisional ball* becomes the *ball in play* **under penalty of stroke and distance** (Rule 27-1).

If the original ball is *lost* outside a *water hazard* or is *out of bounds*, the *provisional ball* becomes the *ball in play*, **under penalty of stroke and distance** (Rule 27-1).

If there is reasonable evidence that the original ball is *lost* in a *water hazard*, the player must proceed in accordance with Rule 26-1.

Exception: If there is reasonable evidence that the original ball is *lost* in an *obstruction* (Rule 24-3) or an *abnormal ground condition* (Rule 25-1c) the player may proceed under the applicable *Rule*.

c. When Provisional Ball to be Abandoned

If the original ball is neither *lost* nor *out of bounds*, the player must abandon the *provisional ball* and continue play with the original ball. If he makes any further *strokes* at the *provisional ball*, he is playing a *wrong ball* and the provisions of Rule 15 apply.

Note: If a player plays a *provisional ball* under Rule 27-2a, the *strokes* made after this Rule has been invoked with a *provisional ball* subsequently abandoned under Rule 27-2c and *penalty strokes* incurred solely by playing that ball are disregarded.

RULE 27 INCIDENT

As described in the Rule 10 Incident [page 48], Phil Mickelson and Frank Lickliter ran into a troublesome situation at the third playoff hole of the 2001 Buick Invitational at Torrey Pines.

First Mickelson and then Lickliter played their drives into a rough canyon to the left of the 17th hole. Each then played a provisional ball in case their original ball was lost in the canyon.

Lickliter's first ball was soon found requiring him to abandon his provisional ball in the fairway. [Rule 27-2c.] After inspecting his lie, he decided that his best course of action was to declare his ball unplayable and replay from the tee, as was his first option under the unplayable ball rule. [Rule 28a.]

Watching events unfold and preferring his chances already lying three in the fairway with his provisional ball, Mickelson asked that the search stop for his original ball in the canyon. "Don't find it," directed Mickelson. "I don't want to find it." He understood that under the Rules a ball cannot be declared lost.

A diligent spotter in the canyon never understood the request, continued his search, and was successful in locating Mickelson's original ball. Fuming at the turn of events, Mickelson could be heard to say, "Did I not ask him to get out of there?"

By Decision 27-2/2, the marshal was obligated to inform Mickelson that his ball was found even though Mickelson preferred to continue with his provisional ball. By Decision 27/13, Mickelson was obligated to identify the found ball and, by Rule 27-2c, to abandon his provisional and continue play with the original ball.

Because his provisional ball was nearer the hole than his original ball was likely to be, had Mickelson played a stroke with his provisional ball before the original was found, the provisional ball would have become the ball in play.

However, with his original ball found, Mickelson was required to deal with its circumstances just as Lickliter had been required to deal with his. Both players' drives were found, both players' provisional balls had to be abandoned, and both declared their balls unplayable and returned to the tee to play their third strokes.

Mickelson, the defending champion, ultimately won with a double bogey six.

RULE **28**

BALL UNPLAYABLE

DEFINITIONS

All defined terms are in *italics* and are listed alphabetically in the Definitions section – see pages 6–15.

See **incident** involving Rule 28 on page 123–124

The player may deem his ball unplayable at any place on the *course* except when the ball is in a *water hazard*. The player is the sole judge as to whether his ball is unplayable.

If the player deems his ball to be unplayable, he must, **under penalty of one stroke**:

121

BALL UNPLAYABLE IN BUNKER: PLAYER'S OPTIONS

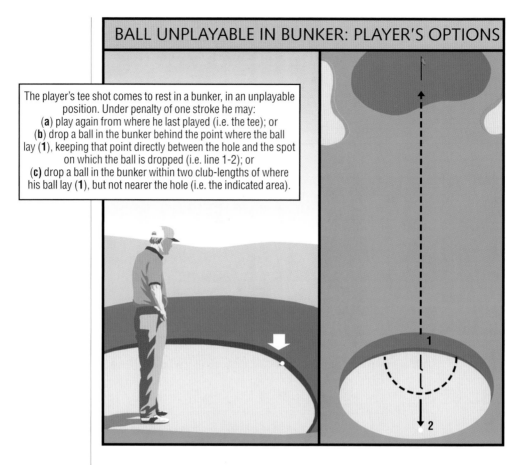

The player's tee shot comes to rest in a bunker, in an unplayable position. Under penalty of one stroke he may:
(**a**) play again from where he last played (i.e. the tee); or
(**b**) drop a ball in the bunker behind the point where the ball lay (**1**), keeping that point directly between the hole and the spot on which the ball is dropped (i.e. line 1-2); or
(**c**) drop a ball in the bunker within two club-lengths of where his ball lay (**1**), but not nearer the hole (i.e. the indicated area).

BALL UNPLAYABLE IN BUSH: PLACE FOR DROPPING

My ball was in the bush. I've declared it unplayable, and I'm going to invoke option **c** and drop the ball within two club-lengths of where it lay.

That's O.K. But remember the ball when dropped must strike a part of the course within two club-lengths of where it lay.

a. Play a ball as nearly as possible at the spot from which the original ball was last played (see Rule 20-5); or

b. Drop a ball behind the point where the ball lay, keeping that point directly between the *hole* and the spot on which the ball is dropped, with no limit to how far behind that point the ball may be dropped; or

c. Drop a ball within two club-lengths of the spot where the ball lay, but not nearer the *hole*.

If the unplayable ball is in a *bunker*, the player may proceed under Clause a, b or c. If he elects to proceed under Clause b or c, a ball must be dropped in the *bunker*.

The ball may be lifted and cleaned when proceeding under this Rule.

PENALTY FOR BREACH OF RULE:
Match play – Loss of hole; Stroke play – Two strokes.

RULE 28 INCIDENT

A ball may be declared unplayable anywhere upon the course except in a water hazard. However, whether a ball lies in a bunker can have an important impact upon the player's options, as Corey Pavin discovered at the 1992 U.S. Open at Pebble Beach.

While it is a question of fact as to where a ball actually lies upon the course, it sometimes takes close inspection to be certain. At the 11th hole,

Pavin's ball found its way under the grassy lip of a fairway bunker. At such a position it was not readily evident whether it was in the bunker or through the green.

The definition of a bunker excludes the grass-covered ground bordering or within the hazard. The margin of the bunker extends vertically downwards but not upward, and a ball is in a bunker when it lies in or any part of it touches the bunker.

By asking for a ruling, Pavin wanted to determine where he was permitted to drop his ball under the provisions of Rule 28. If his ball were not in the bunker, he would be permitted to drop outside the bunker under penalty of one stroke. If his ball were in the bunker, his only dropping option would be within the bunker unless he proceeded under stroke and distance.

After close examination, it was ruled that the ball was in the bunker. Pavin declared it unplayable and dropped in the hazard, keeping the point where the ball lay directly between the hole and the spot on which the ball was dropped. He incurred one penalty stroke.

RULE **29** THREESOMES AND FOURSOMES

DEFINITIONS

All defined terms are in *italics* and are listed alphabetically in the Definitions section – see pages 6–15.

See **incident** involving Rule 29 on page 126

29-1. GENERAL

In a *threesome* or a *foursome*, during any *stipulated round* the *partners* must play alternately from the *teeing grounds* and alternately during the play of each hole. *Penalty strokes* do not affect the order of play.

FOURSOMES: ORDER OF PLAY WHEN PARTNER DRIVES OUT OF BOUNDS

FOURSOMES: WHICH PARTNER DROPS BALL

ORDER OF PLAY IN 36-HOLE COMPETITION

29-2. MATCH PLAY

If a player plays when his *partner* should have played, **his *side* loses the hole**.

29-3. STROKE PLAY

If the *partners* play a *stroke* or *strokes* in incorrect order, such *stroke* or *strokes* are cancelled and **the *side* incurs a penalty of two strokes**. The *side* must correct the error by playing a ball in correct order as nearly as possible at the spot from which it first played in incorrect order (see Rule 20-5). If the *side* makes a *stroke* on the next *teeing ground* without first correcting the error or, in the case of the last hole of the round, leaves the *putting green* without declaring its intention to correct the error, **the *side* is disqualified**.

RULE 29 INCIDENT

The practice putting green at the Old Course in St. Andrews lies just off the course and a short distance from the 1st tee. Paired together on the second day for the morning foursomes of the 1975 Walker Cup Match, the U.S. side of veteran William C. Campbell and newcomer John Grace reported to the tee a little ahead of time. They had already decided that Grace would drive at the odd numbered holes, so Campbell decided to use the extra time before the match to hit a few putts on the practice green some 50 yards from the first tee.

As the visiting team, Campbell and Grace had the honor. The wind was gusting from the west, which carried the announcement of the match's beginning beyond Campbell's earshot.

As the breeze momentarily died, Campbell heard "the click" of Grace's drive just before striking a practice putt, and he was unable to interrupt his stroke. He had practiced during the play of the hole. Instantly and instinctively recognizing his violation, Campbell walked onto the fairway and reported his violation to the referee, the U.S. had just lost the first hole. [Rule 7-2 and Rule 29.]

The referee for the match, John Pasquill from the Royal and Ancient Golf Club, accepted Campbell's report but made no immediate announcement to the other players. Because play of the hole had ended with the Rules violation and the loss of hole, Campbell was free to play his side's second from where Grace's good drive lay to the green, as simply more practice. Besides, he was reluctant to chill his partner's enthusiasm.

Walking across the Swilken Burn, Campbell told Grace what had taken place. "He was incredulous, to say the least," Campbell recalls.

The fact that the practice green was off the course, beyond the out of bounds markers, gave Grace reason to believe they might have a chance on appeal, though there is no such distinction within the Rules.

Campbell reported to Pasquill that his partner wished to protest the ruling and appeal to the Committee. In a neutral voice, Pasquill appropriately replied, "On the golf course, I am the Committee." Thus the Americans lost the first hole and eventually the match to Mark James and Richard Eyles.

RULE  30 | THREE-BALL, BEST-BALL AND FOUR-BALL MATCH PLAY

DEFINITIONS

All defined terms are in *italics* and are listed alphabetically in the Definitions section – see pages 6–15.

30-1. RULES OF GOLF APPLY

The Rules of Golf, so far as they are not at variance with the following specific Rules, apply to *three-ball*, *best-ball* and *four-ball matches*.

30-2. THREE-BALL MATCH PLAY
a. Ball at Rest Moved by an Opponent

Except as otherwise provided in the *Rules*, if the player's ball is touched or *moved* by an opponent, his *caddie* or *equipment* other than during search, Rule 18-3b applies. **That opponent incurs a penalty of one stroke in his match with the player**, but not in his match with the other opponent.

b. Ball Deflected or Stopped by an Opponent Accidentally

If a player's ball is accidentally deflected or stopped by an opponent, his *caddie* or *equipment*, there is no penalty. In his match with that opponent the player may play the ball as it lies or, before another *stroke* is played by either *side*, he may cancel the *stroke* and play a ball without penalty as nearly as possible at the spot from which the original ball was last played (see Rule 20-5). In his match with the other opponent, the ball must be played as it lies.

Exception: Ball striking person attending *flagstick* – see Rule 17-3b.
(Ball purposely deflected or stopped by opponent – see Rule 1-2)

BREACH OF RULE BY ONE PARTNER IN MATCH PLAY

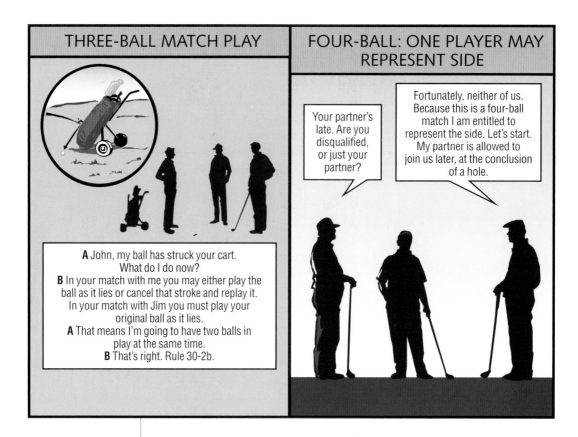

| THREE-BALL MATCH PLAY | FOUR-BALL: ONE PLAYER MAY REPRESENT SIDE |

Your partner's late. Are you disqualified, or just your partner?

Fortunately, neither of us. Because this is a four-ball match I am entitled to represent the side. Let's start. My partner is allowed to join us later, at the conclusion of a hole.

A John, my ball has struck your cart. What do I do now?
B In your match with me you may either play the ball as it lies or cancel that stroke and replay it. In your match with Jim you must play your original ball as it lies.
A That means I'm going to have two balls in play at the same time.
B That's right. Rule 30-2b.

30-3. BEST-BALL AND FOUR-BALL MATCH PLAY

a. Representation of Side

A *side* may be represented by one *partner* for all or any part of a match: all *partners* need not be present. An absent *partner* may join a match between holes, but not during play of a hole.

b. Maximum of 14 Clubs

The *side* **is penalized** for a breach of Rules 4-3a(iii) and 4-4 by any *partner*.

c. Order of Play

Balls belonging to the same *side* may be played in the order the *side* considers best.

d. Wrong Ball

If a player makes a *stroke* at a *wrong ball* that is not in a *hazard*, **he is disqualified for that hole**, but his *partner* incurs no penalty even if the *wrong ball* belongs to him. If the *wrong ball* belongs to another player, its owner must place a ball on the spot from which the *wrong ball* was first played.

e. Disqualification of Side

(i) **A *side* is disqualified** for a breach of any of the following by any *partner*:

Rule 1-3	Agreement to Waive Rules
Rule 4-1 or -2	Clubs
Rule 5-1 or -2	The Ball
Rule 6-2a	Handicap (playing off higher handicap)

Rule 6-4	*Caddie* (having more than one caddie; failure to correct breach immediately)
Rule 6-7	Undue Delay; Slow Play (repeated offense)
Rule 14-3	Artificial Devices and Unusual Equipment

(ii) A *side* is disqualified for a breach of any of the following by all *partners*:

| Rule 6-3 | Time of Starting and Groups |
| Rule 6-8 | Discontinuance of Play |

(iii) In all other cases where a breach of a *Rule* would result in disqualification, **the player is disqualified for that hole only.**

f. Effect of Other Penalties

If a player's breach of a *Rule* assists his *partner's* play or adversely affects an opponent's play, **the *partner* incurs the applicable penalty in addition to any penalty incurred by the player.**

In all other cases where a player incurs a penalty for breach of a *Rule*, the penalty does not apply to his *partner*. Where the penalty is stated to be loss of hole, the effect is to disqualify the player for that hole.

g. Another Form of Match Played Concurrently

In a *best-ball* or *four-ball* match when another form of match is played concurrently, the above specific Rules apply.

RULE 31 FOUR-BALL STROKE PLAY

DEFINITIONS

All defined terms are in *italics* and are listed alphabetically in the Definitions section – see pages 6–15.

31-1. GENERAL

In *four-ball* stroke play two *competitors* play as *partners*, each playing his own ball. The lower score of the *partners* is the score for the hole. If one *partner* fails to complete the play of a hole, there is no penalty.

The Rules of Golf, so far as they are not at variance with the following specific Rules, apply to *four-ball* stroke play.

31-2. REPRESENTATION OF SIDE

A *side* may be represented by either *partner* for all or any part of a *stipulated round*; both *partners* need not be present. An absent *competitor* may join his *partner* between holes, but not during play of a hole.

31-3. MAXIMUM OF 14 CLUBS

The *side* is penalized for a breach of Rules 4-3a (iii) and 4-4 by either *partner*.

31-4. SCORING

The *marker* is required to record for each hole only the gross score of whichever *partner's* score is to count. The gross scores to count must be individually identifiable; otherwise **the *side* is disqualified**. Only one of the *partners* need be responsible for complying with Rule 6-6b.

(Wrong score – see Rule 31-7a)

FOUR BALL STROKE PLAY

Date __3RD APRIL 1996__

Competition __SPRING OPEN FOUR-BALL__

PLAYER A __J. SUTHERLAND__   Handicap __16__   Strokes __12__

PLAYER B __W. B. TAYLOR__   Handicap __12__   Strokes __9__

Hole	Length Yards	Par	Stroke Index	Gross Score A	Gross Score B	Net Score A	Net Score B	Won X Lost – Half O	Mar. Score
1	437	4	4			4	3		
2	320	4	14			4	4		
3	162	3	18			4	4		
4	504	5	7	6		5			
5	181	3	16	4		4			
6	443	4	2	5			4		
7	390	4	8	5			4		
8	346	4	12	5		4			
9	340	4	10	4			3		
Out	3123	35				35			

Hole	Length Yards	Par	Stroke Index	Gross Score A	Gross Score B	Net Score A	Net Score B	Won X Lost – Half O	Mar. Score
10	425	4	3	5		4			
11	141	3	17	3		3			
12	476	5	9	6		5			
13	211	3	11		4	4			
14	437	4	5		5	4			
15	460	4	1		5	4			
16	176	3	15	4		4			
17	340	4	13		4	4			
18	435	4	6	6		5			
In	3101	34				37			
Out	3123	35				35			
T'tl	6224	69				72			

Handicap

Net Score

Player's Signature __J. Sutherland__

Marker's Signature __R. J. Parker__

PARTNERS' SCORES TO BE INDIVIDUALLY IDENTIFIED

1. The lower score of the partners is the score for the hole (Rule 31-1)

2. Only one of the partners need be responsible for complying with Rule 6-6b i.e. recording scores, checking scores, countersigning and returning the card (Rule 31-4).

3. The competitor is solely responsible for the correctness of the gross score recorded. Although there is no objection to the competitor (or his marker) entering the net score, it is the Committee's responsibility to record the better ball score for each hole, to add up the scores and to apply the handicaps recorded on the card (Rule 33-5). Thus there is no penalty for an error by the competitor (or his marker) for recording an incorrect net score.

4. Scores of the two partners must be kept in separate columns otherwise it is impossible for the Committee to apply the correct handicap. If the scores of both partners, having different handicaps, are recorded in the same column, the Committee has no alternative but to disqualify both partners (Rules 31-7 and 6-6 apply).

5. The Committee is responsible for laying down the conditions under which a competition is to be played (Rule 33-1), including the method of handicapping. In the above illustration the Committee laid down that 75% handicaps would apply.

31-5. ORDER OF PLAY

Balls belonging to the same *side* may be played in the order the *side* considers best.

31-6. WRONG BALL

If a *competitor* makes a stroke at a *wrong ball* that is not in a *hazard*, **he incurs a penalty of two strokes** and must correct his mistake by playing the correct ball or by proceeding under the *Rules*. His *partner* incurs no penalty even if the *wrong ball* belongs to him.

   If the *wrong ball* belongs to another *competitor*, its owner must place a ball on the spot from which the *wrong ball* was first played.

31-7. DISQUALIFICATION PENALTIES

a. Breach by One Partner

A *side* is disqualified from the competition for a breach of any of the following by either *partner*:

Rule 1-3	Agreement to Waive *Rules*
Rule 3-4	Refusal to Comply with *Rule*
Rule 4-1 or -2	Clubs
Rule 5-1 or -2	The Ball
Rule 6-2b	Handicap (playing off higher handicap; failure to record handicap)
Rule 6-4	*Caddie* (having more than one caddie; failure to correct breach immediately)
Rule 6-6b	Signing and Returning Score Card
Rule 6-6d	Wrong Score for Hole, i.e., when the recorded score of the *partner* whose score is to count is lower than actually taken. If the recorded score of the *partner* whose score is to count is higher than actually taken, it must stand as returned
Rule 6-7	Undue Delay; Slow Play (repeated offense)
Rule 7-1	Practice Before or Between Rounds
Rule 14-3	Artificial Devices and Unusual Equipment
Rule 31-4	Gross Scores to Count Not Individually Identifiable

b. Breach by Both Partners

A *side* is disqualified:
(i)   for a breach by both of Rule 6-3 (Time of Starting and Groups) or Rule 6-8 (Discontinuance of Play), or
(ii) if, at the same hole, each *partner* is in breach of a *Rule* the penalty for which is disqualification from the competition or for a hole

c. For the Hole Only

In all other cases where a breach of a *Rule* would result in disqualification, **the *competitor* is disqualified only for the hole at which the breach occurred.**

31-8. EFFECT OF OTHER PENALTIES

If a *competitor's* breach of a *Rule* assists his *partner's* play, **the *partner* incurs the applicable penalty in addition to any penalty incurred by the *competitor*.**

   In all other cases where a *competitor* incurs a penalty for breach of a *Rule*, the penalty does not apply to his *partner*.

RULE **32** | # BOGEY, PAR AND STABLEFORD COMPETITIONS

DEFINITIONS

All defined terms are in *italics* and are listed alphabetically in the Definitions section – see pages 6–15.

32-1. CONDITIONS

Bogey, par and Stableford competitions are forms of stroke play in which play is against a fixed score at each hole. The *Rules* for stroke play, so far as they are not at variance with the following specific Rules, apply.

a. Bogey and Par Competitions

The scoring for bogey and par competitions is made as in match play. Any hole for which a *competitor* makes no return is regarded as a loss. The winner is the *competitor* who is most successful in the aggregate of holes.

The *marker* is responsible for marking only the gross number of *strokes* for each hole where the *competitor* makes a net score equal to or less than the fixed score.

Note 1: Maximum of 14 Clubs – Penalties as in match play – see Rule 4-4.
Note 2: One Caddie at Any One Time – Penalties as in match play – see Rule 6-4
Note 3: Undue Delay; Slow Play (Rule 6-7) – The *competitor's* score is adjusted by deducting one hole from the overall result.

b. Stableford Competitions

The scoring in Stableford competitions is made by points awarded in relation to a fixed score at each hole as follows:

Hole Played In	Points
More than one over fixed score or no score returned	0
One over fixed score	1
Fixed score	2
One under fixed score	3
Two under fixed score	4
Three under fixed score	5
Four under fixed score	6

The winner is the *competitor* who scores the highest number of points.

The *marker* is responsible for marking only the gross number of *strokes* at each hole where the *competitor's* net score earns one or more points.

Note 1: Maximum of 14 Clubs (Rule 4-4) – Penalties applied as follows: From total points scored for the round, deduction of two points for each hole at which any breach occurred; maximum deduction per round: four points.
Note 2: One Caddie at Any One Time (Rule 6-4) – Penalties applied as follows: From the points scored for the round; deduction of two points for each hole at which any breach occurred; maximum deduction per round: four points.
Note 3: Undue Delay; Slow Play (Rule 6-7) – The *competitor's* score is adjusted by deducting two points from the total points scored for the round.

32-2. DISQUALIFICATION PENALTIES
a. From the Competition
A *competitor* is disqualified from the competition for a breach of any of the following:

Rule 1-3	Agreement to Waive *Rules*
Rule 3-4	Refusal to Comply with *Rule*
Rule 4-1 or -2	Clubs
Rule 5-1 or -2	The Ball
Rule 6-2b	Handicap (playing off higher handicap; failure to record handicap)
Rule 6-3	Time of Starting and Groups
Rule 6-4	*Caddie* (having more than one caddie; failure to correct breach immediately)
Rule 6-6b	Signing and Returning Card
Rule 6-6d	Wrong Score for Hole, i.e. when the recorded score is lower than actually taken, except that no penalty is incurred when a breach of this Rule does not affect the result of the hole
Rule 6-7	Undue Delay; Slow Play (repeated offense)
Rule 6-8	Discontinuance of Play
Rule 7-1	Practice Before or Between Rounds
Rule 14-3	Artificial Devices and Unusual Equipment

b. For a Hole
In all other cases where a breach of a *Rule* would result in disqualification, **the competitor is disqualified only for the hole at which the breach occurred**.

RULE

THE COMMITTEE

See **incident** involving Rule 33-1 on page 136

DEFINITIONS

All defined terms are in *italics* and are listed alphabetically in the Definitions section – see pages 6–15.

33-1. CONDITIONS; WAIVING RULE
The *Committee* must establish the conditions under which a competition is to be played.

The *Committee* has no power to waive a Rule of Golf.

Certain specific *Rules* governing stroke play are so substantially different from those governing match play that combining the two forms of play is not practicable and is not permitted. The results of *matches* played and the scores returned in these circumstances must not be accepted.

In stroke play the *Committee* may limit a *referee's* duties.

33-2. THE COURSE
a. Defining Bounds and Margins
The *Committee* must define accurately:
(i) the *course* and *out of bounds*,
(ii) the margins of *water hazards* and *lateral water hazards*,
(iii) *ground under repair*, and
(iv) *obstructions* and integral parts of the *course*.

133

b. New Holes

New *holes* should be made on the day on which a stroke play competition begins and at such other times as the *Committee* considers necessary, provided all *competitors* in a single round play with each *hole* cut in the same position.

Exception: When it is impossible for a damaged *hole* to be repaired so that it conforms with the Definition, the *Committee* may make a new *hole* in a nearby similar position.

Note: Where a single round is to be played on more than one day, the *Committee* may provide in the conditions of a competition that the *holes* and *teeing grounds* may be differently situated on each day of the competition, provided that, on any one day, all *competitors* play with each *hole* and each *teeing ground* in the same position.

c. Practice Ground

Where there is no practice ground available outside the area of a competition *course*, the *Committee* should establish the area on which players may practice on any day of a competition, if it is practicable to do so. On any day of a stroke play competition, the *Committee* should not normally permit practice on or to a *putting green* or from a *hazard* of the competition *course*.

d. Course Unplayable

If the *Committee* or its authorized representative considers that for any

If the course is not in a playable condition, the Committee may have to temporarily suspend play. In stroke play only, if further play becomes impossible, the Committee may have to declare play null and void.

reason the *course* is not in a playable condition or that there are circumstances that render the proper playing of the game impossible, it may, in match play or stroke play, order a temporary suspension of play or, in stroke play, declare play null and void and cancel all scores for the round in question. When a round is cancelled, all penalties incurred in that round are cancelled.(Procedure in discontinuing and resuming play – see Rule 6-8.)

33-3. TIMES OF STARTING AND GROUPS

The *Committee* must establish the times of starting and, in stroke play, arrange the groups in which *competitors* must play.

When a match play competition is played over an extended period, the *Committee* establishes the limit of time within which each round must be completed. When players are allowed to arrange the date of their match within these limits, the *Committee* should announce that the match must be played at a stated time on the last day of the period unless the players agree to a prior date.

33-4. HANDICAP STROKE TABLE

The *Committee* must publish a table indicating the order of holes at which handicap *strokes* are to be given or received.

33-5. SCORE CARD

In stroke play, the *Committee* must provide each *competitor* with a score card containing the date and the *competitor's* name or, in *foursome* or *four-ball* stroke play, the *competitors'* names.

In stroke play, the *Committee* is responsible for the addition of scores and application of the handicap recorded on the score card.

In *four-ball* stroke play, the *Committee* is responsible for recording the better-ball score for each hole and in the process applying the handicaps recorded on the score card, and adding the better-ball scores.

In bogey, par and Stableford competitions, the *Committee* is responsible for applying the handicap recorded on the score card and determining the result of each hole and the overall result or points total.

Note: The *Committee* may request that each *competitor* records the date and his name on his score card.

33-6. DECISION OF TIES

The *Committee* must announce the manner, day and time for the decision of a halved match or of a tie, whether played on level terms or under handicap.

A halved match must not be decided by stroke play. A tie in stroke play must not be decided by a match.

33-7. DISQUALIFICATION PENALTY; COMMITTEE DISCRETION

A penalty of disqualification may in exceptional individual cases be waived, modified or imposed if the *Committee* considers such action warranted.

Any penalty less than disqualification must not be waived or modified.

If a *Committee* considers that a player is guilty of a serious breach of etiquette, it may impose a penalty of disqualification under this Rule.

135

See **incident** involving Rule 33-8 below

33-8. LOCAL RULES

a. Policy

The *Committee* may establish Local Rules for local abnormal conditions if they are consistent with the policy set forth in Appendix I.

b. Waiving or Modifying a Rule

A Rule of Golf must not be waived by a Local Rule. However, if a *Committee* considers that local abnormal conditions interfere with the proper playing of the game to the extent that it is necessary to make a Local Rule that modifies the Rules of Golf, the Local Rule must be authorized by the USGA.

RULE 33 INCIDENT

Prior to the opening round of the second U.S. Open, the USGA's first president, Theodore Havemeyer, made what is arguably the most important ruling in the championship's long history.

The championship was held during July 1896 at Shinnecock Hills Golf Club on Long Island and was precluded by a situation which led Havemeyer to establish the Committee's unequivocal authority, as stated in Rule 33, to lay down the conditions under which a competition is to be played.

Gathering before the opening round, a group of competitors, comprised of proficient or professional players mostly from Scotland, England, and private clubs in New York, New England and Chicago, objected to John Shippen being accepted into the competitive field. Shippen's mother was a Shinnecock Indian and his father was a black, Presbyterian minister on the nearby Shinnecock Indian Reservation.

The objectors threatened that, if forced to play with Shippen, they would withdraw from the competition, thereby leaving a weaker field and a dubious U.S. Open champion. At this early point in the game's history in the U.S., those less knowledgeable of the game generally deferred to those proficient at playing it to help mold competitive policies and procedures. Such a dilemma extended to golf in the 1890s. Fortunately, Havemeyer provided insight and direction on his side of the equation.

He met with the objectors and made the USGA's argument succinctly: An open competition was to be held; in order to be an open competition, applications had been accepted from all qualified individuals; to limit the field on any basis would invalidate the open nature of the competition and, in turn, the identification of the national open champion.

Havemeyer emphasized that it was the objectors' unquestioned right to decide whether or not they would compete. However, as far as the national championship was concerned, if Shippen chose to play and he were the only competitor in the field, Shippen would be the national champion.

Feeling the intransigence of Havemeyer's argument and his irrefutable logic, those objecting reversed themselves and chose to compete. James Foulis, a Scottish professional playing out of the Chicago Golf Club was the champion with a score of 152. Shippen tied for fifth.

RULE **34**

DISPUTES AND DECISIONS

DEFINITIONS

All defined terms are in *italics* and are listed alphabetically in the Definitions section – see pages 6–15.

34-1. CLAIMS AND PENALTIES
a. Match Play

If a claim is lodged with the *Committee* under Rule 2-5, a decision should be given as soon as possible so that the state of the match may, if necessary, be adjusted. If a claim is not made in accordance with Rule 2-5, it must not be considered by the *Committee*.

There is no time limit on applying the disqualification penalty for a breach of Rule 1-3.

See **incident**
involving
Rule 34-1b
on page 138

b. Stroke Play

In stroke play, a penalty must not be rescinded, modified or imposed after the competition has closed. A competition is closed when the result has been officially announced or, in stroke play qualifying followed by match play, when the player has teed off in his first match.

Exceptions: A penalty of disqualification must be imposed after the competition has closed if a *competitor*:

(i)   was in breach of Rule 1-3 (Agreement to Waive Rules); or
(ii)   returned a score card on which he had recorded a handicap that, before the competition closed, he knew was higher than that to which he was entitled, and this affected the number of strokes received (Rule 6-2b); or
(iii)   returned a score for any hole lower than actually taken (Rule 6-6d) for any reason other than failure to include a penalty which, before the competition closed, he did not know he had incurred; or
(iv)   knew, before the competition closed, that he had been in breach of any other *Rule* for which the penalty is disqualification.

34-2. REFEREE'S DECISION

If a *referee* has been appointed by the *Committee*, his decision is final.

34-3. COMMITTEE'S DECISION

In the absence of a *referee*, any dispute or doubtful point on the *Rules* must be referred to the *Committee*, whose decision is final.

If the *Committee* cannot come to a decision, it may refer the dispute or doubtful point to the Rules of Golf Committee of the USGA, whose decision is final.

If the dispute or doubtful point has not been referred to the Rules of Golf Committee, the player or players may request that an agreed statement be referred through a duly authorized representative of the *Committee* to the Rules of Golf Committee for an opinion as to the correctness of the decision given. The reply will be sent to this authorized representative.

If play is conducted other than in accordance with the Rules of Golf, the Rules of Golf Committee will not give a decision on any question.

RULE 34 INCIDENT

A case involving Mark O'Meara at the 1997 Lancôme Trophy provided a good example of the operation of Rule 34-1b. Video evidence came to light a considerable time after the competition had closed which demonstrated that during the final round O'Meara, having marked and lifted his ball on the putting green, mistakenly and unknown to himself, replaced his ball in a wrong place marginally closer to the hole.

If O'Meara's error had been noticed prior to the player returning his card, O'Meara would have been penalised two strokes at the hole concerned for playing from a wrong place (Rule 20-7b). If the breach had come to light after O'Meara had returned his card, but prior to the competition closing, the Committee would have had no choice but to disqualify him under Rule 6-6d as his score for the hole was lower than actually taken due to failure to include the penalty.

However, Rule 34-1b provides that except in the four situations listed under the Rule, the Committee may not impose, rescind or modify a penalty after the competition has closed and, as O'Meara's mistake came to light after the result of the competition had been announced this meant that no penalty was imposed by the Committee. The results stood as played, with O'Meara the winner of the Tournament by one stroke.

APPENDIX I

CONTENTS

APPENDIX I INCIDENT

The development of different configurations of golf balls, particularly since the 1980s, introduced a predicament to competitive golf that was previously unimportant. Hard balls might go farther and be of greater assistance on long holes, while softer balls provided more control that might be valued on shorter holes.

The idea that a competitor might change golf balls depending on what was demanded at a particular hole runs contrary to the idea that a round is to be played with one unalterable set of equipment. Clubs cannot be altered or interchanged, so why should the ball vary?

Setting the conditions of the competition is one of the responsibilities of the Committee. Part C of Appendix I of the Rules of Golf brings attention to a number of specific matters that may need consideration by the Committee. One of these is called the One Ball Condition. If adopted, the so-called "one-ball rule" states that the balls a player uses during a stipulated round must be of the same brand and type. [Appendix I, Part C, b.]

Even at major championships, with the world's leading players and caddies competing, mistakes of the simplest nature can occur. During the first round of the 2003 U.S. Open, Niclas Fasth ran afoul of the one-ball rule. The 7th hole at Olympia Fields is a downhill par-3. The walking path around the green runs below the putting surface. Following the players' tee shots, as the walking Rules Official with Fasth's game took the path around the green, his eyes were at a level nearly equal to that of Fasth's ball lying just on the back fringe. Indeed, attempting to determine if the ball was on or off the green brought the ball under closer scrutiny.

The ball type Fasth had chosen on the first hole of the round was a black Callaway, which was a rare type at the time. When the walking official glanced across the green from the path, he noticed that Fasth's ball in play was a red Callaway. Rather than distract Fasth during the play of the hole, the official decided to let him finish the hole with the red Callaway, as permitted under the Local Rule, and then address the apparent infraction.

Fasth putted from the fringe to within a few feet of the hole. He then walked to his ball and leaned over in order to mark, lift and clean it. At that moment, the difference in ball types registered a startled look on Fasth's face. He looked around for the rules official in order to resolve the situation.

Once the switch was discovered, the pertinent question was where had it taken place. If it had been on the 7th tee, two penalty strokes would be assessed. If it had happened before that, the maximum of four strokes would be the penalty.

"We discussed it at the completion of the hole," recalls Bob Hooper, the walking rules official. "Niclas and his caddie were both sure it had happened on the 7th tee and not before. He switched back to the black Callaway, and completed the round." Once the round was completed, Fasth and his caddie were asked to review the incident again to be certain the switch had not taken place before the 7th tee. They were certain and that was good enough for all concerned.

PART A LOCAL RULES

As provided in Rule 33-8a, the *Committee* may make and publish Local Rules for local abnormal conditions if they are consistent with the policy established in this Appendix. In addition, detailed information regarding acceptable and prohibited Local Rules is provided in "Decisions on the Rules of Golf" under Rule 33-8 and in "How to Conduct a Competition."

If local abnormal conditions interfere with the proper playing of the game and the *Committee* considers it necessary to modify a Rule of Golf, authorization from the USGA must be obtained.

1. DEFINING BOUNDS AND MARGINS

Specifying means used to define *out of bounds, water hazards, lateral water hazards, ground under repair, obstructions* and integral parts of the *course* (Rule 33-2a).

2. WATER HAZARDS

a. Lateral Water Hazards
Clarifying the status of *water hazards* that may be *lateral water hazards* (Rule 26).

b. Provisional Ball
Permitting play of a *provisional ball* under Rule 26-1 for a ball that may be in a *water hazard* of such character that if the original ball is not found, there is reasonable evidence that it is *lost* in the *water hazard* and it would be impracticable to determine whether the ball is in the *hazard* or to do so would unduly delay play. The ball is played provisionally under any of the available options under Rule 26-1 or any applicable Local Rule. In such a case, if a *provisional ball* is played and the original ball is in a *water hazard*, the player may play the original ball as it lies or continue with the *provisional ball* in play, but he may not proceed under Rule 26-1 with regard to the original ball.

3. AREAS OF THE COURSE REQUIRING PRESERVATION; ENVIRONMENTALLY-SENSITIVE AREAS

Assisting preservation of the *course* by defining areas, including turf nurseries, young plantations and other parts of the *course* under cultivation as *"ground under repair"* from which play is prohibited.

When the *Committee* is required to prohibit play from environmentally-sensitive areas that are on or adjoin the *course*, it should make a Local Rule clarifying the relief procedure.

4. TEMPORARY CONDITIONS – MUD, EXTREME WETNESS, POOR CONDITIONS AND PROTECTION OF COURSE

a. Lifting an Embedded Ball, Cleaning
Temporary conditions that might interfere with proper playing of the game, including mud and extreme wetness, warranting relief for an embedded ball anywhere *through the green* or permitting lifting, cleaning and replacing a ball anywhere *through the green* or on a closely-mown area *through the green*.

b. "Preferred Lies" and "Winter Rules"
Adverse conditions, including the poor condition of the *course* or the existence of mud, are sometimes so general, particularly during winter months, that the *Committee* may decide to grant relief by temporary Local Rule either to protect the *course* or to promote fair and pleasant play. The Local Rule must be withdrawn as soon as the conditions warrant.

5. OBSTRUCTIONS

a. General
Clarifying status of objects that may be *obstructions* (Rule 24).

Declaring any construction to be an integral part of the *course* and, accordingly, not an *obstruction*, e.g., built-up sides of *teeing grounds*, *putting greens* and *bunkers* (Rules 24 and 33-2a).

b. Stones in Bunkers
Allowing the removal of stones in *bunkers* by declaring them to be "movable *obstructions*" (Rule 24-1).

c. Roads and Paths
(i)   Declaring artificial surfaces and sides of roads and paths to be integral parts of the *course*, or
(ii) Providing relief of the type afforded under Rule 24-2b from roads and paths not having artificial surfaces and sides if they could unfairly affect play.

d. Immovable Obstructions Close to Putting Green
Providing relief from intervention by immovable *obstructions* on or within two club-lengths of the *putting green* when the ball lies within two club-lengths of the *obstruction*.

e. Protection of Young Trees
Providing relief for the protection of young trees.

f. Temporary Obstructions
Providing relief from interference by temporary *obstructions* (e.g., grandstands, television cables and equipment, etc).

6. DROPPING ZONES (BALL DROPS)

Establishing special areas on which balls may or must be dropped when it is not feasible or practicable to proceed exactly in conformity with Rule 24-2b or 24-3 (*Immovable Obstruction*), Rule 25-1b or 25-1c (*Abnormal Ground Conditions*), Rule 25-3 (*Wrong Putting Green*), Rule 26-1 (*Water Hazards* and *Lateral Water Hazards*) or Rule 28 (*Ball Unplayable*).

PART B SPECIMEN LOCAL RULES

Within the policy established in Part A of this Appendix, the *Committee* may adopt a Specimen Local Rule by referring, on a score card or notice board, to the examples given below. However, Specimen Local Rules 3a, 3b, 3c, 6a and 6b, should not be printed or referred to on a score card as they are all of limited duration.

1. AREAS OF THE COURSE REQUIRING PRESERVATION; ENVIRONMENTALLY-SENSITIVE AREAS

a. Ground Under Repair; Play Prohibited

If the *Committee* wishes to protect any area of the *course*, it should declare it to be *ground under repair* and prohibit play from within that area. **The following Local Rule is recommended:**
"The _____(defined by ____) is *ground under repair* from which play is prohibited. If a player's ball lies in the area, or if it interferes with the player's *stance* or the area of his intended swing, the player must take relief under Rule 25-1.

PENALTY FOR BREACH OF LOCAL RULE:
Match play – Loss of hole;
Stroke play – Two strokes."

b. Environmentally-Sensitive Areas

If an appropriate authority (i.e. a Government Agency or the like) prohibits entry into and/or play from an area on or adjoining the *course* for environmental reasons, the *Committee* should make a Local Rule clarifying the relief procedure.

The *Committee* has some discretion in terms of whether the area is defined as *ground under repair*, a *water hazard* or *out of bounds*. However, it may not simply define the area to be a *water hazard* if it does not meet the Definition of a "*Water Hazard*" and it should attempt to preserve the character of the hole. **The following Local Rule is recommended:**

"I. Definition

An environmentally-sensitive area is an area so declared by an appropriate authority, entry into and/or play from which is prohibited for environmental reasons. These areas may be defined as *ground under repair*, a *water hazard*, a *lateral water hazard* or *out of bounds* at the discretion of the *Committee* provided that, in the case of an environmentally-sensitive area which has been defined as a *water hazard* or a *lateral*

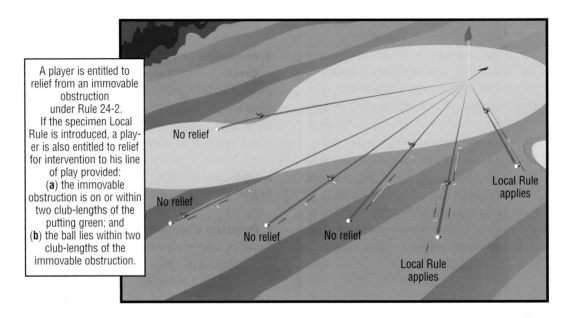

A player is entitled to relief from an immovable obstruction under Rule 24-2.
If the specimen Local Rule is introduced, a player is also entitled to relief for intervention to his line of play provided:
(**a**) the immovable obstruction is on or within two club-lengths of the putting green; and
(**b**) the ball lies within two club-lengths of the immovable obstruction.

No relief

No relief

No relief   No relief

Local Rule applies

Local Rule applies

The Links course at Spanish Bay in California has areas of sand dunes which have been declared environmentally-sensitive. A player may not play from or enter these areas.

water hazard, the area is, by Definition, a *water hazard*.

Note: The *Committee* may not declare an area to be environmentally-sensitive.

II. Ball in Environmentally-Sensitive Area
a. Ground Under Repair

If a ball is in an environmentally-sensitive area that is defined as *ground under repair*, a ball must be dropped in accordance with Rule 25-1b.

If there is reasonable evidence that a ball is *lost* within an environmentally-sensitive area that is defined as *ground under repair*, the player may take relief without penalty as prescribed in Rule 25-1c.

b. Water Hazards and Lateral Water Hazards

If a ball is in or there is reasonable evidence that it is *lost* in an environmentally-sensitive area that is defined as a *water hazard* or *lateral water hazard*, the player must, under penalty of one stroke, proceed under Rule 26-1.

Note: If a ball, dropped in accordance with Rule 26 rolls into a position where the environmentally-sensitive area interferes with the player's *stance* or the area of his intended swing, the player must take relief as provided in Clause III of this Local Rule.

c. Out of Bounds

If a ball is in an environmentally-sensitive area that is defined as *out of bounds*, the player

must play a ball, under penalty of one stroke, as nearly as possible at the spot from which the original ball was last played (see Rule 20-5).

III. Interference with Stance or Area of Intended Swing

Interference by an environmentally-sensitive area occurs when the condition interferes with the player's *stance* or the area of his intended swing. If interference exists, the player must take relief as follows:

(i) **Through the Green:** If the ball lies *through the green*, the point on the *course* nearest to where the ball lies must be determined that (a) is not nearer the *hole*, (b) avoids interference by the condition and (c) is not in a *hazard* or on a *putting green*. The player must lift the ball and drop it without penalty within one club-length of the point so determined on a part of the *course* that fulfills (a), (b) and (c) above.

(ii) **In a Hazard:** If the ball is in a *hazard*, the player must lift the ball and drop it either:
(a) Without penalty, in the *hazard*, as near as possible to the spot where the ball lay, but not nearer the *hole*, on a part of the *course* that provides complete relief from the condition; or
(b) **Under penalty of one stroke**, outside the *hazard*, keeping the point where the ball lay directly between the *hole* and the spot on which the ball is dropped, with no limit to how far behind the *hazard* the ball may be dropped.

Additionally, the player may proceed under Rule 26 or 28 if applicable

(iii) **On the Putting Green:** If the ball lies on the *putting green*, the player must lift the ball and place it without penalty in the nearest position to where it lay that affords complete relief from the condition, but not nearer the *hole* or in a *hazard*. The ball may be cleaned when lifted under Clause III of this Local Rule.

Exception: A player may not obtain relief under Clause III of this Local Rule if (a) it is clearly unreasonable for him to make a *stroke* because of interference by anything other than a condition covered by this Local Rule or (b) interference by the condition would occur only through use of an unnecessarily abnormal *stance*, swing or direction of play.

PENALTY FOR BREACH OF LOCAL RULE:
Match play – Loss of hole;
Stroke play – Two strokes.

Note: In the case of a serious breach of this Local Rule, the *Committee* may impose a penalty of disqualification."

2. PROTECTION OF YOUNG TREES

When it is desired to prevent damage to young trees, **the following Local Rule is recommended**:

"Protection of young trees identified by _____ – If such a tree interferes with a player's *stance* or the area of his intended swing, the ball must be lifted, without penalty, and dropped in accordance with the procedure prescribed in Rule 24-2b (Immovable *Obstruction*). If the ball lies in a *water hazard*, the player must lift and drop the ball in accordance with Rule 24-2b(i) except that the *nearest point of relief* must be in the *water hazard* and the ball must be dropped in the *water hazard* or the player may proceed under Rule 26. The ball may be cleaned when lifted under this Local Rule.

Exception: A player may not obtain relief under this Local Rule if (a) it is clearly unreasonable for him to make a *stroke* because of interference by anything other than the tree or (b) interference by the tree would occur only through use of an unnecessarily abnormal *stance*, swing or direction of play.

PENALTY FOR BREACH OF LOCAL RULE:
Match play – Loss of hole;
Stroke play – Two strokes."

3. TEMPORARY CONDITIONS – MUD, EXTREME WETNESS, POOR CONDITIONS AND PROTECTION OF THE COURSE

a. Relief for Embedded Ball; Cleaning Ball

Rule 25-2 provides relief without penalty for a ball embedded in its own pitch-mark in any closely-mown area *through the green*. On the *putting green*, a ball may be lifted and damage caused by the impact of a ball may be repaired (Rules 16-1b and c). When permission to take relief for an embedded ball anywhere *through the green* would be warranted, **the following Local Rule is recommended**:

"*Through the green*, a ball that is embedded in its own pitch-mark in the ground, other than sand, may be lifted without penalty, cleaned and dropped as near as possible to where it lay but not nearer the *hole*. The ball when dropped must first strike a part of the *course through the green*.

Exception: A player may not obtain relief under this Local Rule if it is clearly unreasonable for him to make a *stroke* because of interference by anything other than the condition covered by this Local Rule.

PENALTY FOR BREACH OF LOCAL RULE:
Match play – Loss of hole;
Stroke play – Two strokes."

Alternatively, conditions may be such that permission to lift, clean and replace the ball will suffice. In these circumstances, **the following Local Rule is recommended**:

"(Specify area) a ball may be lifted, cleaned and replaced without penalty.

Note: The position of the ball must be marked before it is lifted under this Local Rule – see Rule 20-1.

PENALTY FOR BREACH OF LOCAL RULE:
Match play – Loss of hole;
Stroke play – Two strokes."

b. "Preferred Lies" and "Winter Rules"

Occasional local abnormal conditions that might interfere with fair play and are not widespread

should be defined as *ground under repair*.

However, adverse conditions, such as heavy snows, spring thaws, prolonged rains or extreme heat can make fairways unsatisfactory and sometimes prevent use of heavy mowing equipment. When such conditions are so general throughout a *course* that the *Committee* believes "preferred lies" or "winter rules" would promote fair play or help protect the *course*, **the following Local Rule is recommended**:

"A ball lying on a closely-mown area *through the green* [or specify a more restricted area, e.g. at the 6th hole] may be lifted without penalty and cleaned. Before lifting the ball, the player must mark its position. Having lifted the ball, he must place it on a spot within [specify area, e.g. six inches, one club-length, etc.] of and not nearer the *hole* than where it originally lay, that is not in a *hazard* and not on a *putting green*.

A player may place his ball only once, and it is in play when it has been placed (Rule 20-4). If the ball fails to come to rest on the spot on which it is placed, Rule 20-3d applies. If the ball when placed comes to rest on the spot on which it is placed and it subsequently *moves*, there is

no penalty and the ball must be played as it lies, unless the provisions of any other *Rule* apply.

If the player fails to mark the position of the ball before lifting it or *moves* the ball in any other manner, such as rolling it with a club, he incurs a penalty of one stroke.

*PENALTY FOR BREACH OF LOCAL RULE
Match play – Loss of hole;
Stroke play – Two strokes

*If a player incurs the general penalty for a breach of this Local Rule, no additional penalty under the Local Rule is applied."

c. Aeration Holes

When a *course* has been aerated, a Local Rule permitting relief, without penalty, from an aeration hole may be warranted. **The following Local Rule is recommended**:

"*Through the green*, a ball that comes to rest in or on an aeration hole may be lifted without penalty, cleaned and dropped, as near as possible to the spot where it lay but not nearer the *hole*. The ball when dropped must first strike a part of the *course through the green*.

On the *putting green*, a ball that comes to rest in or on an aeration hole may be placed at the

145

nearest spot not nearer the *hole* that avoids the situation.

4. STONES IN BUNKERS

Stones are, by definition, *loose impediments* and, when a player's ball is in a *hazard*, a stone lying in or touching the *hazard* may not be touched or moved (Rule 13-4). However, stones in *bunkers* may represent a danger to players (a player could be injured by a stone struck by the player's club in an attempt to play the ball) and they may interfere with the proper playing of the game.

When permission to lift a stone in a *bunker* would be warranted, **the following Local Rule is recommended**:

"Stones in *bunkers* are movable *obstructions* (Rule 24-1 applies)."

5. IMMOVABLE OBSTRUCTIONS CLOSE TO PUTTING GREEN

Rule 24-2 provides relief without penalty from interference by an immovable *obstruction*, but it also provides that, except on the *putting green*, intervention on the *line of play* is not, of itself, interference under this Rule.

However, on some courses, the aprons of the *putting greens* are so closely mown that players may wish to putt from just off the green. In such conditions, immovable *obstructions* on the apron may interfere with the proper playing of the game and the introduction of **the following Local Rule providing additional relief without penalty from intervention by an immovable *obstruction* would be warranted**:

"Relief from interference by an immovable *obstruction* may be obtained under Rule 24-2. In addition, if a ball lies off the *putting green* but not in a *hazard* and an immovable *obstruction* on or within two club-lengths of the *putting green* and within two club-lengths of the ball intervenes on the *line of play* between the ball and the *hole*, the player may take relief as follows:

The ball must be lifted and dropped at the nearest point to where the ball lay that (a) is not nearer the *hole*, (b) avoids intervention and (c) is not in a *hazard* or on a *putting green*. The ball may be cleaned when lifted.

Relief under this Local Rule is also available if the player's ball lies on the *putting green* and an immovable *obstruction* within two club-lengths of the *putting green* intervenes on his *line of putt*. The player may take relief as follows: The ball must be lifted and placed at the nearest point where the ball lay that (a) is not nearer the *hole*, (b) avoids intervention and (c) is not in a *hazard*. The ball may be cleaned when lifted.

6. TEMPORARY OBSTRUCTIONS

When temporary *obstructions* are installed on or adjoining the *course*, the *Committee* should define the status of such *obstructions* as movable, immovable or temporary immovable *obstructions*.

a. Temporary Immovable Obstructions

If the *Committee* defines such *obstructions* as temporary immovable *obstructions*, **the following Local Rule is recommended**:

"I. Definition

A temporary immovable *obstruction* is a non-permanent artificial object that is often erected in conjunction with a competition and is fixed or not readily movable.

Examples of temporary immovable *obstructions* include, but are not limited to, tents, scoreboards, grandstands, television towers and lavatories.

Supporting guy wires are part of the temporary immovable *obstruction* unless the *Committee* declares that they are to be treated as elevated power lines or cables.

II. Interference

Interference by a temporary immovable *obstruction* occurs when (a) the ball lies in front of and so close to the *obstruction* that the *obstruction* interferes with the player's *stance* or the area of his intended swing, or (b) the ball lies in, on, under or behind the *obstruction* so that any part of the *obstruction* intervenes directly between the player's ball and the *hole*;

interference also exists if the ball lies within one club-length of a spot equidistant from the hole where such intervention would exist.

Note: A ball is under a temporary immovable *obstruction* when it is below the outer most edges of the obstruction, even if these edges do not extend downwards to the ground.

III. Relief

A player may obtain relief from interference by a temporary immovable *obstruction*, including a temporary immovable *obstruction* that is *out of bounds*, as follows:

(a) **Through the Green:** If the ball lies *through the green*, the point on the *course* nearest to where the ball lies must be determined that (a) is not nearer the *hole*, (b) avoids interference as defined in Clause II and (c) is not in a *hazard* or on a *putting green*. The player must lift the ball and drop it without penalty within one club-length of the point so determined on a part of the *course* that fulfills (a), (b) and (c) above.

(b) **In a Hazard:** If the ball is in a *hazard*, the player must lift and drop the ball either:
(i) Without penalty, in accordance with Clause IIIa above, except that the nearest part of the *course* affording complete relief must be in the *hazard* and the ball must be dropped in the *hazard* or, if complete relief is impossible, on a part of the *course* within the *hazard* that affords maximum available relief; or
(ii) Under penalty of one stroke, outside the *hazard* as follows: the point on the *course* nearest to where the ball lies must be determined that (a) is not nearer the *hole*, (b) avoids interference as defined in Clause II and (c) is not in a *hazard*. The player must drop the ball within one club-length of the point so determined on a part of the *course* that fulfills (a), (b) and (c) above.

The ball may be cleaned when lifted under Clause III.

Note 1: If the ball lies in a *hazard*, nothing in this Local Rule precludes the player from proceeding under Rule 26 or Rule 28, if applicable.

Note 2: If a ball to be dropped under this Local Rule is not immediately recoverable, another ball may be *substituted*.

Note 3: A *Committee* may make a Local Rule (a) permitting or requiring a player to use a dropping zone or ball drop when taking relief from a temporary immovable *obstruction* or (b) permitting a player, as an additional relief option, to drop the ball on the opposite side of the *obstruction* from the point established under Clause III, but otherwise in accordance with Clause III.

Exceptions: If a player's ball lies in front of or behind the temporary immovable *obstruction* (not in, on or under the *obstruction*) he may not obtain relief under Clause 3 if:

1. It is clearly unreasonable for him to make a *stroke* or, in the case of intervention, to make a *stroke* such that the ball could finish on a direct line to the *hole*, because of interference by anything other than the temporary immovable *obstruction*;
2. Interference by the temporary immovable *obstruction* would occur only through use of an unnecessarily abnormal *stance*, swing or direction of play; or
3. In the case of intervention, it would be clearly unreasonable to expect the player to be able to strike the ball far enough towards the *hole* to reach the temporary immovable *obstruction*.

Note: A player not entitled to relief due to these exceptions may proceed under Rule 24-2, if applicable

IV. Ball Lost

If there is reasonable evidence that the ball is *lost* in, on or under a temporary immovable *obstruction*, a ball may be dropped under the provisions of Clause III or Clause V, if applicable.

For the purpose of applying Clauses III and V, the ball is deemed to lie at the spot where it last crossed the outermost limits of the *obstruction* (Rule 24-3).

V. Dropping Zones (Ball Drops)

If the player has interference from a temporary immovable *obstruction*, the *Committee* may permit or require the use of a dropping zone or ball drop. If the player uses a dropping zone in taking relief, he must drop the ball in the dropping zone nearest to where his ball originally lay or is deemed to lie under Clause

147

If there are temporary immovable obstructions, such as TV towers, on the course, the Committee should introduce a Local Rule providing for relief from such temporary immovable obstructions.

IV (even though the nearest dropping zone may be nearer the *hole*).

Note 1: A *Committee* may make a Local Rule prohibiting the use of a dropping zone or ball drop that is nearer the *hole*.

Note 2: If the ball is dropped in a dropping zone, the ball must not be re-dropped if it comes to rest within two club-lengths of the spot where it first struck a part of the *course* even though it may come to rest nearer the *hole* or outside the boundaries of the dropping zone.

PENALTY FOR BREACH OF LOCAL RULE:

Match play – Loss of hole;
Stroke play – Two strokes."

b. Temporary Power Lines and Cables

When temporary power lines, cables, or telephone lines are installed on the *course*, **the following Local Rule is recommended:**

"Temporary power lines, cables, telephone lines and mats covering or stanchions supporting them are *obstructions*:

1. If they are readily movable, Rule 24-1 applies.
2. If they are fixed or not readily movable, the player may, if the ball lies *through the green* or in a *bunker*, obtain relief as provided in Rule 24-2b. If the ball lies in a *water hazard*, the player may lift and drop the ball in accordance with Rule 24-2b(i) except that the *nearest point of relief* must be in the *water hazard* and the ball must be dropped in the *water hazard* or the player may proceed under

Rule 26.

3. If a ball strikes an elevated power line or cable, the *stroke* must be cancelled and replayed, without penalty (see Rule 20-5). If the ball is not immediately recoverable another ball may be *substituted*.

    Note: Guy wires supporting a temporary immovable *obstruction* are part of the temporary immovable *obstruction* unless the *Committee*, by Local Rule, declares that they are to be treated as elevated power lines or cables.

    Exception: Ball striking elevated junction section of cable rising from the ground must not be replayed.

4. Grass-covered cable trenches are *ground under repair* even if not marked and Rule 25-1b applies."

PART C CONDITIONS OF THE COMPETITION

Rule 33-1 provides, "The *Committee* must establish the conditions under which a competition is to be played." The conditions should include many matters such as method of entry, eligibility, number of rounds to be played, etc. which it is not appropriate to deal with in the Rules of Golf or this Appendix. Detailed information regarding these conditions is provided in "Decisions on the Rules of Golf" under Rule 33-1 and in "How to Conduct a Competition."

However, there are a number of matters that might be covered in the Conditions of the Competition to which the *Committee's* attention is specifically drawn. These are:

1. SPECIFICATION OF THE BALL (NOTE TO RULE 5-1)

The following two conditions are recommended only for competitions involving expert players:

a. List of Conforming Golf Balls

The USGA periodically issues a List of Conforming Golf Balls which lists balls that have been tested and found to conform. If the *Committee* require players to play a brand of golf ball on the List, the List should be posted and **the following condition of competition used:**

"The ball the player plays must be named on the

current List of Conforming Golf Balls issued by the USGA.

PENALTY FOR BREACH OF CONDITION:
Disqualification."

b. One Ball Condition

If it is desired to prohibit changing brands and types of golf balls during a *stipulated round*, **the following condition is recommended:**

"Limitation on Balls Used During Round: (Note to Rule 5-1)

(i) "One Ball" Condition

During a *stipulated round*, the balls a player plays must be of the same brand and type as detailed by a single entry on the current List of Conforming Golf Balls.

Note: If a ball of a different brand and/or type is dropped or placed it may be lifted, without penalty, and the player must then proceed by dropping or placing a proper ball (Rule 20-6).

PENALTY FOR BREACH OF CONDITION:
Match Play – At the conclusion of the hole at which the breach is discovered, the state of the match must be adjusted by deducting one hole for each hole at which a breach occurred; maximum deduction per round: Two holes.
Stroke Play – Two strokes for each hole at which any breach occurred; maximum penalty per round: Four strokes.

(ii) Procedure When Breach Discovered

When a player discovers that he has played a ball in breach of this condition, he must abandon that ball before playing from the next *teeing ground* and complete the round with a proper ball; otherwise, the player is disqualified. If discovery is made during play of a hole and the player elects to *substitute* a proper ball before completing that hole, the player must place a proper ball on the spot where the ball played in breach of the condition lay."

2. TIME OF STARTING
(NOTE TO RULE 6-3A)

If the *Committee* wishes to act in accordance with the Note, **the following wording is recommended:**

"If the player arrives at his starting point, ready to play, within five minutes after his starting time, in the absence of circumstances that warrant waiving the penalty of disqualification as provided in Rule 33-7, the penalty for failure to start on time is loss of the first hole to be played in match play or two strokes in stroke play. Penalty for lateness beyond five minutes is disqualification."

3. CADDIE
(NOTE TO RULE 6-4)

Rule 6-4 permits a player to use a *caddie* provided he has only one *caddie* at any one time. However, there may be circumstances where a *Committee* may wish to ban *caddies* or restrict a player in his choice of *caddie*, e.g. professional golfer, sibling, parent, another player in the competition, etc. In such cases, **the following wording is recommended:**
Use of Caddie Prohibited

"A player is prohibited from using a *caddie* during the *stipulated round*."
Restriction on Who May Serve as Caddie

"A player is prohibited from having _____ serve as his *caddie* during the *stipulated round*."

PENALTY FOR BREACH OF CONDITION:
Match play – At the conclusion of the hole at which the breach is discovered, the state of the match is adjusted by deducting one hole for each hole at which a breach occurred; maximum deduction per round – Two holes.
Stroke play – Two strokes for each hole at which any breach occurred; maximum penalty per round – Four strokes.
Match or stroke play – In the event of a breach between the play of two holes, the penalty applies to the next hole.
A player having a *caddie* in breach of this condition must immediately upon discovery that a breach has occurred ensure that he conforms with this condition for the remainder of the *stipulated round*. Otherwise, the player is disqualified.

4. PACE OF PLAY
(NOTE 2 TO RULE 6-7)

The *Committee* may establish pace of play guidelines to help prevent slow play, in accordance with Note 2 to Rule 6-7.

149

5. SUSPENSION OF PLAY DUE TO A DANGEROUS SITUATION (NOTE TO RULE 6-8B)

As there have been many deaths and injuries from lightning on golf courses, all clubs and sponsors of golf competitions are urged to take precautions for the protection of persons against lightning. Attention is called to Rules 6-8 and 33-2d. If the *Committee* desires to adopt the condition in the Note under Rule 6-8b, **the following wording is recommended:**

"When play is suspended by the *Committee* for a dangerous situation, if the players in a match or group are between the play of two holes, they must not resume play until the *Committee* has ordered a resumption of play. If they are in the process of playing a hole, they must discontinue play immediately and not resume play until the *Committee* has ordered a resumption of play. If a player fails to discontinue play immediately, he is disqualified unless circumstances warrant waiving the penalty as provided in Rule 33-7.

The signal for suspending play due to a dangerous situation will be a prolonged note of the siren."

The following signals are generally used and it is recommended that all *Committees* do similarly:
Discontinue Play Immediately: One prolonged note of siren.
Discontinue Play: Three consecutive notes of siren, repeated.
Resume Play: Two short notes of siren, repeated.

6. PRACTICE

a. General

The *Committee* may make regulations governing practice in accordance with the Note to Rule 7-1, Exception (c) to Rule 7-2, Note 2 to Rule 7 and Rule 33-2c.

b. Practice Between Holes (Note 2 to Rule 7)

It is recommended that a condition of competition prohibiting practice putting or chipping on or near the *putting green* of the hole last played be introduced only in stroke play competitions.

The following wording is recommended:

"A player must not play any practice *stroke* on or near the *putting green* of the hole last played. If a practice *stroke* is played on or near the *putting green* of the hole last played, the player

150

incurs a penalty of two strokes at the next hole, except that in the case of the last hole of the round, he incurs the penalty at that hole."

7. ADVICE IN TEAM COMPETITIONS (NOTE TO RULE 8)

If the *Committee* wishes to act in accordance with the Note under Rule 8, **the following wording is recommended:**

"In accordance with the Note to Rule 8 of the Rules of Golf, each team may appoint one person (in addition to the persons from whom *advice* may be asked under that Rule) who may give *advice* to members of that team. Such person (if it is desired to insert any restriction on who may be nominated insert such restriction here) must be identified to the *Committee* before giving *advice*."

8. NEW HOLES (NOTE TO RULE 33-2B)

The *Committee* may provide, in accordance with the Note to Rule 33-2b, that the *holes* and *teeing grounds* for a single round competition, being held on more than one day, may be differently situated on each day.

9. TRANSPORTATION

If it is desired to require players to walk in a competition, **the following condition is recommended:**

"Players must walk at all times during a *stipulated round*.

PENALTY FOR BREACH OF CONDITION:
Match play – At the conclusion of the hole at which the breach is discovered, the state of the match must be adjusted by deducting one hole for each hole at which a breach occurred.
Maximum deduction per round: Two holes.
Stroke play – Two strokes for each hole at which any breach occurred; maximum penalty per round: Four strokes. In the event of a breach between the play of two holes, the penalty applies to the next hole.
Match or stroke play – Use of any unauthorized form of transportation must be discontinued immediately upon discovery that a breach has occurred. Otherwise, the player is disqualified."

10. ANTI-DOPING

The *Committee* may require, in the Conditions of Competition, that players comply with an anti-doping policy.

11. HOW TO DECIDE TIES

Rule 33-6 empowers the *Committee* to determine how and when a halved match or a stroke play tie is decided. The decision should be published in advance.

The USGA recommends:

Match Play

A match which ends all square should be played off hole by hole until one *side* wins a hole. The play-off should start on the hole where the match began. In a handicap match, handicap strokes should be allowed as in the prescribed round.

Stroke Play

(a) In the event of a tie in a scratch stroke play competition, a play-off is recommended. Such a play-off may be over 18 holes or a smaller number of holes as specified by the *Committee*. If that is not feasible or there is still a tie, a hole-by-hole play-off is recommended.

(b) In the event of a tie in a handicap stroke play competition, a play-off with handicaps is recommended. Such a play-off may be over 18 holes or a smaller number of holes as specified by the *Committee*. If the play-off is less than 18 holes the percentage of 18 holes to be played should be applied to the players' handicaps to determine their play-off handicaps. Handicap stroke fractions of one-half stroke or more should count as a full stroke and any lesser fraction should be disregarded.

(c) In either a scratch or handicap stroke play competition, if a play-off of any type is not feasible, matching score cards is recommended. The method of matching cards should be announced in advance. An acceptable method of matching cards is to determine the winner on the basis of the best score for the last nine holes. If the tying players have the same score for the last nine, determine the winner on the basis of the last six holes, last three holes and finally the 18th hole. If this method is used in a handicap stroke play competition, one-half, one-third, one-sixth, etc. of the handicaps should be deducted. Fractions should not be disregarded. If this method is used in a competition with a multiple tee start, it is recommended that the "last nine holes, last six holes, etc." is considered to be holes 10-18, 13-18, etc.

(d) If the conditions of the competition provide that ties are to be decided over the last nine, last six, last three and last hole, they should also provide what will happen if this procedure does not produce a winner.

12. DRAW FOR MATCH PLAY

Although the draw for match play may be completely blind or certain players may be distributed through different quarters or eighths, the General Numerical Draw is recommended if matches are determined by a qualifying round.

General Numerical Draw

For purposes of determining places in the draw, ties in qualifying rounds other than those for the last qualifying place are decided by the order in which scores are returned, with the first score to be returned receiving the lowest available number, etc. If it is impossible to determine the order in which scores are returned, ties are determined by a blind draw.

UPPER HALF	LOWER HALF
64 QUALIFIERS	
1 vs. 64	2 vs. 63
32 vs. 33	31 vs. 34
16 vs. 49	15 vs. 50
17 vs. 48	18 vs. 47
8 vs. 57	7 vs. 58
25 vs. 40	26 vs. 39
9 vs. 56	10 vs. 55
24 vs. 41	23 vs. 42
4 vs. 61	3 vs. 62
29 vs. 36	30 vs. 35
13 vs. 52	14 vs. 51
20 vs. 45	19 vs. 46
5 vs. 60	6 vs. 59
28 vs. 37	27 vs. 38
12 vs. 53	11 vs. 54
21 vs. 44	22 vs. 43

UPPER HALF	LOWER HALF
32 QUALIFIERS	
1 vs. 32	2 vs. 31
16 vs. 17	15 vs. 18
8 vs. 25	7 vs. 26
9 vs. 24	10 vs. 23
4 vs. 29	3 vs. 30
13 vs. 20	14 vs. 19
5 vs. 28	6 vs. 27
12 vs. 21	11 vs. 22
16 QUALIFIERS	
1 vs. 16	2 vs.15
8 vs. 9	7 vs.10
4 vs. 13	3 vs.14
5 vs. 12	6 vs. 11
8 QUALIFIERS	
1 vs. 8	2 vs. 7
4 vs. 5	3 vs. 6

APPENDICES II & III

Any design in a club or ball which is not covered by Rules 4 and 5 and Appendices II and III, or which might significantly change the nature of the game, will be ruled on by the United States Golf Association.

The dimensions contained in Appendices II and III are referenced in imperial measurements. A metric conversion is also referenced for information, calculated using a conversion rate of 1 inch = 25.4 mm. In the event of any dispute over the conformity of a club or ball, the imperial measurement takes precedence.

APPENDIX II

DESIGN OF CLUBS

A player in doubt as to the conformity of a club should consult the United States Golf Association.

A manufacturer should submit to the United States Golf Association a sample of a club which is to be manufactured for a ruling as to whether the club conforms with the Rules. If a manufacturer fails to submit a sample or to await a ruling before manufacturing and/or marketing the club, the manufacturer assumes the risk of a ruling that the club does not conform to the Rules. Any sample submitted to the United States Golf Association becomes its property for reference purposes.

The following paragraphs prescribe general regulations for the design of clubs, together with specifications and interpretations. Further information relating to these regulations and their proper interpretation is provided in "A Guide to the Rules on Clubs and Balls."

Where a club, or part of a club, is required to have some specific property, this means that it must be designed and manufactured with the intention of having that property. The finished club or part must have that property within manufacturing tolerances appropriate to the material used.

1. CLUBS
a. General
A club is an implement designed to be used for striking the ball and generally comes in three forms: woods, irons and putters distinguished by shape and intended use. A putter is a club with a loft not exceeding ten degrees designed primarily for use on the putting green.

The club must not be substantially different from the traditional and customary form and make. The club must be composed of a shaft and a head. All parts of the club must be fixed so that the club is one unit, and it must have no external attachments except as otherwise permitted by the Rules.

b. Adjustability
Woods and irons must not be designed to be adjustable except for weight. Putters may be designed to be adjustable for weight and some other forms of adjustability are also permitted. All methods of adjustment permitted by the Rules require that:
(i)   the adjustment cannot be readily made;
(ii)   all adjustable parts are firmly fixed and there is no reasonable likelihood of them working loose during a round; and
(iii) all configurations of adjustment conform with the Rules.
The disqualification penalty for purposely changing the playing characteristics of a club during a stipulated round (Rule 4-2a) applies to all clubs including a putter.

c. Length
The overall length of the club must be at least 18 inches (457.2 mm) and, except for putters, must not exceed 48 inches (1,219.2 mm). For woods and irons the measurement of length is taken when the club is lying on a horizontal plane and the sole is set against a 60 degree plane as

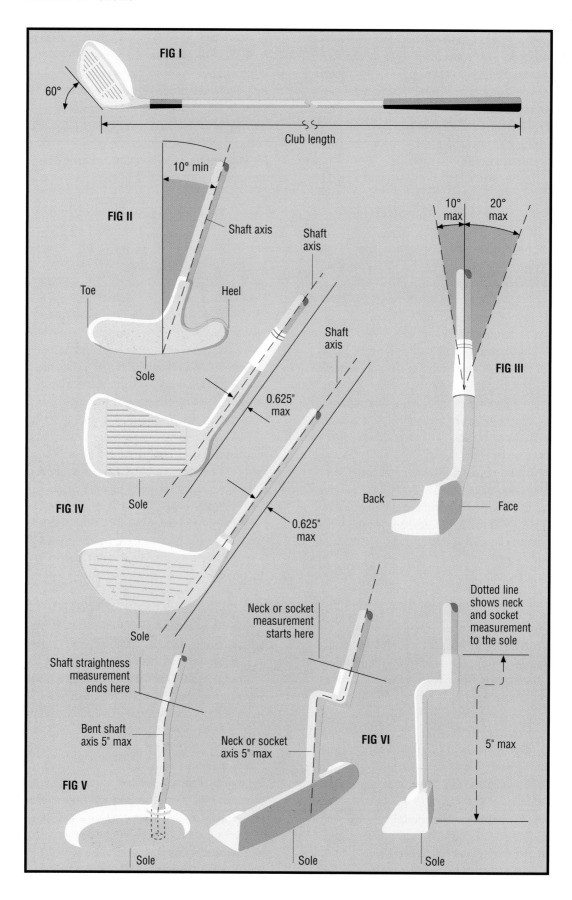

FIG I

60°

Club length

FIG II

10° min

Shaft axis

Toe

Heel

Sole

Shaft axis

Shaft axis

0.625" max

FIG IV

Sole

10° max

20° max

FIG III

Back

Face

Shaft axis

0.625" max

Sole

Neck or socket measurement starts here

Dotted line shows neck and socket measurement to the sole

Shaft straightness measurement ends here

Bent shaft axis 5" max

Neck or socket axis 5" max

FIG VI

5" max

FIG V

Sole

Sole

Sole

shown in Fig. I. The length is defined as the distance from the point of the intersection between the two planes to the top of the grip. For putters, the measurement of length is taken from the top of the grip along the axis of the shaft or a straight line extension of it to the sole of the club.

Note: Clubs in breach of the maximum length limit as specified in Appendix II, 4c, which were in use or marketed prior to January 1, 2004 and which otherwise conform to the Rules, may be used until December 31, 2004.

d. Alignment

When the club is in its normal address position the shaft must be so aligned that:

(i)   the projection of the straight part of the shaft on to the vertical plane through the toe and heel must diverge from the vertical by at least 10 degrees (see Fig. II);

(ii)   the projection of the straight part of the shaft on to the vertical plane along the intended line of play must not diverge from the vertical by more than 20 degrees forwards or 10 degrees backwards (see Fig. III).

Except for putters, all of the heel portion of the club must lie within 0.625 inches (15.88 mm) of the plane containing the axis of the straight part of the shaft and the intended (horizontal) line of play (see Fig. IV).

2. SHAFT

a. Straightness

The shaft must be straight from the top of the grip to a point not more than 5 inches (127 mm) above the sole, measured from the point where the shaft ceases to be straight along the axis of the bent part of the shaft and the neck and/or socket (see Fig. V).

b. Bending and Twisting Properties

At any point along its length, the shaft must:

(i)   bend in such a way that the deflection is the same regardless of how the shaft is rotated about its longitudinal axis; and

(ii)   twist the same amount in both directions.

c. Attachment to Clubhead

The shaft must be attached to the clubhead at the heel either directly or through a single plain neck and/or socket. The length from the top of the neck and/or socket to the sole of the club must not exceed 5 inches (127 mm), measured along the axis of, and following any bend in, the neck and/or socket (see Fig. VI).

Exception for Putters: The shaft or neck or socket of a putter may be fixed at any point in the head.

3. GRIP (see Fig. VII)

The grip consists of material added to the shaft to enable the player to obtain a firm hold. The grip must be straight and plain in form, must extend to the end of the shaft and must not be moulded for any part of the hands. If no material is added, that portion of the shaft designed to be held by the player must be considered the grip.

(i)   For clubs other than putters the grip must be circular in cross-section, except that a continuous, straight, slightly raised rib may be incorporated along the full length of the grip, and a slightly indented spiral is permitted on a wrapped grip or a replica of one.

(ii)   A putter grip may have a non-circular cross-section, provided the cross-section has no concavity, is symmetrical and remains generally similar throughout the length of the grip. (See Clause (v) below).

(iii)   The grip may be tapered but must not have any bulge or waist. Its cross-sectional dimensions measured in any direction must not exceed 1.75 inches (44.45 mm).

(iv)   For clubs other than putters the axis of the grip must coincide with the axis of the shaft.

(v)   A putter may have two grips provided each is circular in cross-section, the axis of each coincides with the axis of the shaft, and they are separated by at least 1.5 inches (38.1mm).

4. CLUBHEAD

a. Plain in Shape

The clubhead must be generally plain in shape. All parts must be rigid, structural in nature and functional. It is not practicable to define plain in shape precisely and comprehensively but features which are deemed to be in breach of this requirement

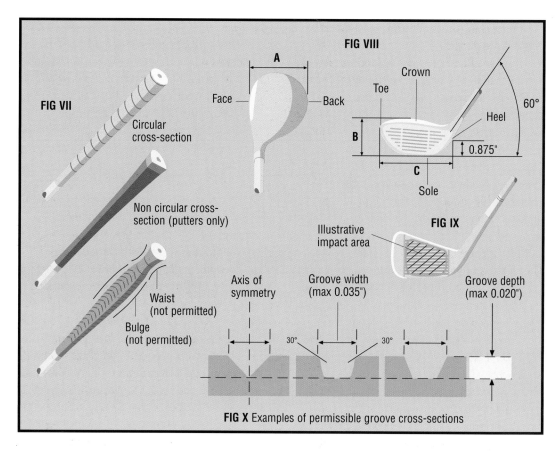

FIG VII

Circular cross-section

Non circular cross-section (putters only)

Waist (not permitted)

Bulge (not permitted)

FIG VIII

A

Face — — Back

Crown

Toe

Heel

B

0.875"

C

Sole

60°

FIG IX

Illustrative impact area

Axis of symmetry

Groove width (max 0.035")

Groove depth (max 0.020")

30° 30°

FIG X Examples of permissible groove cross-sections

and are therefore not permitted include:

(i)   holes through the head,

(ii)   transparent material added for other than decorative or structural purposes,

(iii)   appendages to the main body of the head such as knobs, plates, rods or fins,

for the purpose of meeting dimensional specifications, for aiming or for any other purpose. Exceptions may be made for putters.

Any furrows in or runners on the sole must not extend into the face.

b. Dimensions and Size
(i) Woods

When the club is in a 60 degree lie angle, the dimensions of the clubhead must be such that:

(a)   the distance from the heel to the toe of the clubhead must be greater than the distance from the face to the back;

(b)   the distance from the heel to the toe of the clubhead is not greater than 5 inches (127 mm); and

(c)   the distance from the sole to the crown of the clubhead is not greater than 2.8

inches (71.12 mm).

These dimensions are measured on horizontal lines between vertical projections of the outermost points of:

- the heel and the toe; and
- the face and the back (see Fig. VIII, dimension A);

and on vertical lines between the horizontal projections of the outermost points of the sole and the crown (see Fig. VIII, dimension B). If the outermost point of the heel is not clearly defined, it is deemed to be 0.875 inches (22.23 mm) above the horizontal plane on which the club is lying (see Fig. VIII, dimension C).

The size of the clubhead must not exceed 28.06 cubic inches (460 cubic centimetres), plus a tolerance of 0.61 cubic inches (10 cubic centimetres).

Note: Clubs in breach of the maximum size limit as specified in Appendix II, 4b (i), which were in use or marketed prior to January 1, 2004 and which otherwise conform to the Rules, may be used until December 31, 2004.

(ii) Irons and Putters

When the clubhead is in its normal address position the dimensions of the head must be such that the distance from the heel to the toe is greater than the distance from the face to the back. For traditionally shaped heads, these dimensions will be measured on horizontal lines between vertical projections of the outermost points of:

- the heel and the toe; and
- the face and the back.

For unusually shaped heads, the toe to heel dimension may be made at the face.

c. Striking Faces

The clubhead must have only one striking face, except that a putter may have two such faces if their characteristics are the same, and they are opposite each other.

5. CLUB FACE

a. General

The material and construction of, or any treatment to, the face or clubhead must not have the effect at impact of a spring (test on file), or impart significantly more or less spin to the ball than a standard steel face, or have any other effect which would unduly influence the movement of the ball.

The face of the club must be hard and rigid (some exceptions may be made for putters) and, except for such markings listed below, must be smooth and must not have any degree of concavity.

b. Impact Area Roughness and Material

Except for markings specified in the following paragraphs, the surface roughness within the area where impact is intended (the "impact area") must not exceed that of decorative sandblasting, or of fine milling (see Fig. IX).

The whole of the impact area must be of the same material. Exceptions may be made for wooden clubs.

c. Impact Area Markings

Markings in the impact area must not have sharp edges or raised lips as determined by a finger test. Grooves or punch marks in the impact area must meet the following specifications:

(i) Grooves. A series of straight grooves with diverging sides and a symmetrical cross-section may be used (see Fig. X).

- The width and cross-section must be consistent across the face of the club and along the length of the grooves.
- Any rounding of groove edges must be in the form of a radius which does not exceed 0.020 inches (0.508 mm).
- The width of the grooves must not exceed 0.035 inches (0.9 mm), using the 30 degree method of measurement on file with the United States Golf Association.
- The distance between edges of adjacent grooves must not be less than three times the width of a groove, and not less than 0.075 inches (1.905 mm).
- The depth of a groove must not exceed 0.020 inches (0.508 mm).

Note: Exception – see US Decision 4-1/100

(ii) Punch Marks. Punch marks may be used. The area of any such mark must not exceed 0.0044 square inches (2.84 sq. mm). A mark must not be closer to an adjacent mark than 0.168 inches (4.27 mm) measured from center to center. The depth of a punch mark must not exceed 0.040 inches (1.02 mm). If punch marks are used in combination with grooves, a punch mark must not be closer to a groove than 0.168 inches (4.27 mm), measured from center to center.

d. Decorative Markings

The center of the impact area may be indicated by a design within the boundary of a square whose sides are 0.375 inches (9.53 mm) in length. Such a design must not unduly influence the movement of the ball. Decorative markings are permitted outside the impact area.

e. Non-metallic Club Face Markings

The above specifications apply to clubs on which the impact area of the face is of metal or a material of similar hardness. They do not apply to clubs with faces made of other materials and whose loft angle is 24 degrees or less, but markings which could unduly influence the movement of the ball are prohibited. Clubs with this type of face and a loft angle exceeding 24 degrees may have grooves of maximum width 0.040 inches (1.02 mm) and maximum depth 1½ times the groove width, but must otherwise conform to the markings specifications above.

f. Putter Face Markings
The specifications above with regard to roughness, material and markings in the impact area do not apply to putters.

APPENDIX III

THE BALL

1. WEIGHT
The weight of the ball shall not be greater than 1.620 ounces avoirdupois (45.93 gm).

2. SIZE
The diameter of the ball shall be not less than 1.680 inches (42.67mm). This specification will be satisfied if, under its own weight, a ball falls through a 1.680 inches diameter ring gauge in fewer than 25 out of 100 randomly selected positions, the test being carried out at a temperature of 23 ± 1°C.

3. SPHERICAL SYMMETRY
The ball must not be designed, manufactured or intentionally modified to have properties which differ from those of a spherically symmetrical ball.

4. INITIAL VELOCITY
The initial velocity of the ball shall not exceed the limit specified (test on file) when measured on apparatus approved by the United States Golf Association.

5. OVERALL DISTANCE STANDARD
The combined carry and roll of the ball, when tested on apparatus approved by the United States Golf Association, shall not exceed the distance specified under the conditions set forth in the Overall Distance Standard for golf balls on file with the United States Golf Association.

ACKNOWLEDGEMENTS

Published in 2004
by Hamlyn, an imprint of Octopus Publishing Group Ltd
2–4 Heron Quays, London E14 4JP

Text copyright © 2004 United States Golf Association
Design copyright © 2004 Octopus Publishing Group Ltd

Distributed in the United States and Canada by
Sterling Publishing Co., Inc
387 Park Avenue South, New York, NY 10016-8810

ISBN 0 600 61068 3

Printed in Italy

PHOTOGRAPHIC ACKNOWLEDGEMENTS

Allsport 104 top, / David Cannon 13, 32, 73, 94, top, 115, 119, / Graham Chadwick 115, / Phil Cole 134, / Craig Jones 94 bottom, / Warren Little 44, / Stephen Munday 8 right,/ Andrew Redington 33

Peter Dazeley 104 bottom

Joann Dost Golf Editions / Joann Dost 68 bottom

Royal & Ancient 7

Phil Sheldon Golf Picture Library 8 left, 25, 62, 103, 112, 143, 148

RULES INCIDENTS ACKNOWLEDGEMENT

Gary Galyean